SECOND EDITION

VOLUME ONE
Verna Aardema to Ashley Bryan

Favorite Children's
AUTHORS *and*
ILLUSTRATORS

E. Russell Primm III, Editor in Chief

PO Box 326, Chanhassen, MN 55317-0326
800/599-READ
http://www.childsworld.com

A NOTE TO OUR READERS:

The publication dates listed in each author's or illustrator's selected bibliography represent the date of first publication in the United States.

The editors have listed literary awards that were announced prior to August 2006.

Every effort has been made to contact copyright holders of material included in this reference work. If any errors or omissions have occurred, corrections will be made in future editions.

Photographs ©: Favorite Children's Authors and Illustrators: Volume 1
By E. Russell Primm III, Editor in Chief

Photographs: 10, 134—de Grummond Collection, University of Southern Mississippi; 14, 42, 146—Harcourt; 18—Arnold Adoff; 26—Joan Aiken; 30—Bettmann / Corbis; 34, 130—Penguin Putnam; 54, 66, 122—Scholastic; 58, 118—Houghton Mifflin; 62, 106, 110—HarperCollins; 70—Jim Walker / Lynne Reid Banks; 74—Joan Bauer; 78, 102—Library of Congress; 82—Kerlan Collection, University of Minnesota; 86—Viking Press / Kerlan Collection, University of Minnesota; 90—Jan and Stan Berenstein; 94—Barry Lewis / Alamy; 114—Greenwillow Books / Kerlan Collection, University of Minnesota; 126—Michael Cart; 138—Consuelo Kanaga / HarperCollins; 142—Candlewick Press; 154—Simon & Schuster.

An Editorial Directions book

LIBRARY OF CONGRESS CATALOGING-IN-PUBLICATION DATA

Favorite children's authors and illustrators / E. Russell Primm III, editor-in-chief. — 2nd ed.
    v. cm.
  Includes bibliographical references and index.
  Contents: v. 1. Verna Aardema to Ashley Bryan.
  ISBN-13: 978-1-59187-057-9 (v.1 : alk. paper)
  ISBN-10: 1-59187-057-7 (v. 1 : alk. paper)
  ISBN-13: 978-1-59187-058-6 (v. 2 : alk. paper)
  ISBN-10: 1-59187-058-5 (v. 2 : alk. paper)
  ISBN-13: 978-1-59187-059-3 (v. 3 : alk. paper)
  ISBN-10: 1-59187-059-3 (v. 3 : alk. paper)
  ISBN-13: 978-1-59187-060-9 (v. 4 : alk. paper)
  ISBN-10: 1-59187-060-7 (v. 4 : alk. paper)
  ISBN-13: 978-1-59187-061-6 (v. 5 : alk. paper)
  ISBN-10: 1-59187-061-5 (v. 5 : alk. paper)
  ISBN-13: 978-1-59187-062-3 (v. 6 : alk. paper)
  ISBN-10: 1-59187-062-3 (v. 6 : alk. paper)
  ISBN-13: 978-1-59187-063-0 (v. 7 : alk. paper)
  ISBN-10: 1-59187-063-1 (v. 7 : alk. paper)
  ISBN-13: 978-1-59187-064-7 (v. 8 : alk. paper)
  ISBN-10: 1-59187-064-X (v. 8 : alk. paper)
  1. Children's literature—Bio-bibliography—Dictionaries—Juvenile literature. 2. Young adult literature Bio-bibliography—Dictionaries—Juvenile literature. 3. Illustrators—Biography—Dictionaries—Juvenile literature. 4. Children—Books and reading—Dictionaries—Juvenile literature. 5. Young Adults—Books and reading—Dictionaries—Juvenile literature. I. Primm, E. Russell, 1958–
  PN1009.A1F38 2007
  809'.8928203—dc22
  [B]   2006011358

TABLE OF CONTENTS

INTRODUCTION

by E. Russell Primm III, Editor in Chief

The second edition of Favorite Children's Authors and Illustrators has been expanded by two volumes and is a compendium of nearly 300 biographical essays. The eight volumes of Favorite Children's Authors and Illustrators are a considered cross section of young readers' favorite authors and illustrators from, primarily, the twentieth century. While this is by no means a comprehensive list, it does serve as an excellent introduction to many of those storytellers most beloved by children—from Verna Aardema to Virginia Hamilton, from Julius Lester to Allen Say, from Gary Soto to Charlotte Zolotow.

Student researchers and young readers are motivated not only by the demands of teachers and curriculum, but also by curiosity and a desire to know. They have an affinity for narrative of all kinds and stories of every variety. And they are intrigued by those authors and illustrators responsible for the stories they take to heart. Young readers' natural curiosity about the people behind their favorite books finds satisfaction in biography and autobiography. Biography is surely storytelling at its most personal.

Favorite Children's Authors and Illustrators, Second Edition, was conceived, designed, and constructed with its intended audience of middle-grade readers in mind. Each essay is brief but informative, and the child-pleasing elements are many: most entries include a photograph of the author or illustrator, reproductions of book covers, quotes from and about the subject, and interesting facts. The selected bibliography of each person's work has been completely revised and updated for this second edition, along with the list of suggested resources, both print and online, for further study.

This accessible eight-volume set satisfies the browsing, exploring, and report-writing needs of young readers. The editors hope to receive from both juvenile and adult readers suggestions for individuals to include in the third edition of the set. Suggestions may be sent to:

Editors
Tradition Publishing Company
PO Box 320
Excelsior, MN 55331

Or

authorsandillustrators@editorialdirections.com

MAJOR CHILDREN'S AUTHOR AND ILLUSTRATOR LITERARY AWARDS

THE AMERICAN BOOK AWARDS
Awarded from 1980 to 1983 in place of the National Book Award to give national recognition to achievement in several categories of children's literature

BOSTON GLOBE–HORN BOOK AWARDS
Established in 1967 by Horn Book *magazine and the* Boston Globe *newspaper to honor the year's best fiction, poetry, nonfiction, and picture books for children*

THE CALDECOTT MEDAL
Established in 1938 and presented by the Association for Library Service to Children division of the American Library Association to illustrators for the most distinguished picture book for children from the preceding year

THE CARNEGIE MEDAL
Established in 1936 and presented by the British Library Association for an outstanding book for children written in English

THE CARTER G. WOODSON BOOK AWARDS
Established in 1974 and presented by the National Council for the Social Studies for the most distinguished social science books appropriate for young readers that depict ethnicity in the United States

THE CORETTA SCOTT KING AWARDS
Established in 1970 in connection with the American Library Association to honor African American authors and illustrators whose books are deemed outstanding, educational, and inspirational

THE HANS CHRISTIAN ANDERSEN MEDAL
Established in 1956 by the International Board on Books for Young People to honor an author or illustrator, living at the time of nomination, whose complete works have made a lasting contribution to children's literature

THE KATE GREENAWAY MEDAL

Established by the Youth Libraries Group of the British Library Association in 1956 to honor illustrators of children's books published in the United Kingdom

THE LAURA INGALLS WILDER AWARD

Established by the Association for Library Service to Children division of the American Library Association in 1954 to honor an author or illustrator whose books, published in the United States, have made a substantial and lasting contribution to children's literature

THE MICHAEL L. PRINTZ AWARD

Established by the Young Adult Library Services division of the American Library Association in 2000 to honor literary excellence in young adult literature (fiction, nonfiction, poetry, or anthology)

THE NATIONAL BOOK AWARDS

Established in 1950 to give national recognition to achievement in fiction, nonfiction, poetry, and young people's literature

THE NEWBERY MEDAL

Established in 1922 and presented by the Association for Library Service to Children division of the American Library Association for the most distinguished contribution to children's literature in the preceding year

THE ORBIS PICTUS AWARD FOR OUTSTANDING NONFICTION

Established in 1990 by the National Council of Teachers of English to honor an outstanding informational book published in the preceding year

THE PURA BELPRÉ AWARD

Established in 1996 and cosponsored by the Association for Library Service to Children division of the American Library Association and the National Association to Promote Library Services to the Spanish Speaking to recognize a writer and illustrator of Latino or Latina background whose works affirm and celebrate the Latino experience

THE SCOTT O'DELL AWARD

Established in 1982 and presented by the O'Dell Award Committee to an American author who writes an outstanding tale of historical fiction for children or young adults that takes place in the New World

Verna Aardema

Born: June 6, 1911
Died: May 11, 2000

During her career, Verna Aardema was an elementary schoolteacher and newspaper journalist. She also used her love of storytelling to become an award-winning children's author, writing thirty-three books for children and young people. Her best-known books for children include *Why Mosquitoes Buzz in People's Ears, Rabbit Makes a Monkey of a Lion, Who's in Rabbit's House? and Oh, Kojo! How Could You?* Verna Aardema

was born on June 6, 1911, in New Era, Michigan, the third of nine children in her family. Her mother often needed her help with the other children. But Verna spent most of her time reading books. Her mother had a difficult time getting her to help with the chores. Verna was always more interested in reading than in housework.

As a child, Verna did not feel that she pleased her parents. Because the family was so large, she often

---

AFTER SHE RETIRED FROM TEACHING, AARDEMA VISITED ELEMENTARY SCHOOLS TO TELL STORIES. SHE ALSO GAVE LECTURES TO ASPIRING WRITERS AT COLLEGES AND CONVENTIONS.

went unnoticed. It was not until she was about eleven years old that she impressed her parents. Verna wrote a poem for school and received an A for it. When she brought the poem home to show her parents, they were very excited. Her mother told her that she could become a writer just like her great-grandfather. From that day on, Verna Aardema knew she wanted to be a writer.

> *"Mama knew that I sometimes told stories to the neighborhood kids [back] there in the swamp, [...] [the] [...]ood place [...]m to hatch [...]riter."*

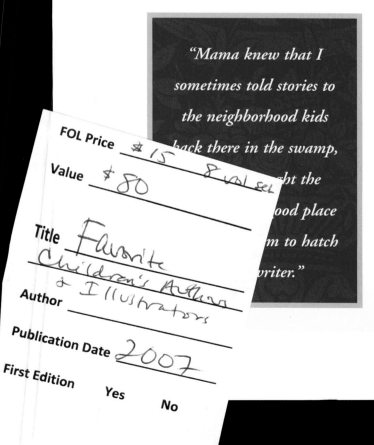

FOL Price $15 8 vol set

Value $80

Title Favorite Children's Authors & Illustrators

Author

Publication Date 2007

First Edition   Yes   No

Why Mosquitoes Buzz in People's Ears
Verna Aardema | pictures by
Leo and Diane Dillon

A Selected Bibliography of Aardema's Work

Koi and the Kola Nuts: A Tale from Liberia (1999)
Anansi Does the Impossible!: An Ashanti Tale (1997)
This for That: A Tonga Tale (1997)
The Lonely Lioness and the Ostrich Chicks: A Masai Tale (1996)
Jackal's Flying Lesson: A Khoikhoi Tale (1995)
Misoso: Once Upon a Time Tales from Africa (1994)
A Bookworm Who Hatched (1993)
Sebgugugu the Glutton: A Bantu Tale from Rwanda (1993)
Anansi Finds a Fool: An Ashanti Tale (1992)
Borreguita and the Coyote: A Tale from Ayutla, Mexico (1991)
Pedro & the Padre: A Tale from Jalisco, Mexico (1991)
Traveling to Tondo: A Tale of the Nkundo of Zaire (1991)
The Vingananee and the Tree Toad: A Liberian Tale (1991)
Rabbit Makes a Monkey of Lion: A Swahili Tale (1989)
Princess Gorilla and a New Kind of Water: A Mpongwe Tale (1988)
Bimwili & the Zimwi: A Tale from Zanzibar (1985)
Oh, Kojo! How Could You! An Ashanti Tale (1984)
What's So Funny, Ketu? A Nuer Tale (1982)
Bringing the Rain to Kapiti Plain: A Nandi Tale (1981)
The Riddle of the Drum: A Tale from Tizapán, Mexico (1979)
Half-a-Ball-of-Kenki: An Ashanti Tale Retold (1979)
Ji-Nongo-Nongo Means Riddles (1978)
Who's in Rabbit's House? A Masai Tale (1977)
Why Mosquitoes Buzz in People's Ears: A West African Tale (1975)
Behind the Back of the Mountain: Black Folktales from Southern Africa (1973)
Tales for the Third Ear, from Equatorial Africa (1969)
More Tales from the Story Hat (1966)
Tales from the Story Hat (1960)

> *"I was a bookworm. But in my household, reading was considered a form of laziness. In my case, it really was. Because in order to get me to help with the housework, they first had to get me away from whatever book I happened to be reading. I was always in trouble over that."*

Verna loved to write stories. Her mother encouraged her to work on her writing. It was difficult for Verna to find a quiet place in the house. She soon discovered a nearby swamp she liked to visit. She would walk to the swamp and sit on the logs. There she spent hours thinking of stories. She also learned that these walks to the swamp were a good way to get out of doing her chores!

After finishing high school, Verna Aardema attended Michigan State University, where she took many writing classes. She even won three writing contests. When she graduated, she took a job as an elementary schoolteacher. Aardema was a teacher for twenty-four years. While she was a teacher, she also worked as a writer for a newspaper in Michigan.

Aardema began writing after her first child was born. Her young daughter would not eat a meal unless her mother told her a story. Aardema made up stories so that her daughter would eat. Because Aardema was interested in Africa, many of the stories she told were African folktales. Her love of storytelling took on a new focus when she

––––

MANY OF AARDEMA'S STORIES INCLUDE ANIMAL CHARACTERS THAT SPEAK USING STRANGE WORDS AND SOUNDS.

published her first book in 1960. That book, *Tales from the Story Hat,* was a collection of African folktales. Aardema went on to write many other books based on African and Mexican folktales.

Aardema died on May 11, 2000. She was eighty-eight years old.

ꙮ

WHERE TO FIND OUT MORE ABOUT VERNA AARDEMA

BOOKS

Aardema, Verna. *A Bookworm Who Hatched.*
Katonah, N.Y.: Owen Publications, 1992.

Berger, Laura Standley, ed. *Twentieth-Century Children's Writers.* 4th ed.
Detroit: St. James Press, 1995.

Collier, Laurie, and Joyce Nakamura, eds.
*Major Authors and Illustrators for Children and Young Adults:
A Selection of Sketches from Something about the Author.*
Detroit: Gale Research, 1993.

McElmeel, Sharron L. *100 Most Popular Picture Book Authors and Illustrators: Biographical Sketches and Bibliographies.* Englewood, Colo.: Libraries Unlimited, 2000.

Sutherland, Zena. *Children and Books.* 9th Ed. New York: Addison-Wesley
Educational Publishers Inc., 1997.

WEB SITES

KIDSPOINT
http://www.kidspoint.org/columns2.asp?column_id=534&column_type=author
Read an excerpt from the biography *The Bookworm Who Hatched*
as well as links to other sites

UNIVERSITY OF SOUTHERN MISSISSIPPI DE GRUMMOND COLLECTION
http://avatar.lib.usm.edu/%7Edegrum/html/research/findaids/aardema.htm
To read an autobiographical sketch and a list of her written works

---

AARDEMA'S *WHY MOSQUITOES BUZZ IN PEOPLE'S EARS,* ILLUSTRATED BY LEO AND DIANE DILLON, WAS AWARDED THE CALDECOTT MEDAL IN 1976.

David A. Adler

Born: April 10, 1947

David A. Adler didn't start off as a writer. Instead, he began his career as a math teacher. Once he began writing, however, Adler knew he had to keep at it. Since 1975, he has written more than 200 books. Some of Adler's books are about serious subjects. Others are just seriously silly. No matter what he's writing about though, one thing's for sure: David Adler knows how to please kids of all ages.

David Adler was born in New York City on April 10, 1947. He grew up in a big house on Long Island, New York. With three brothers and two sisters, Adler remembers a house filled with children. He also remembers having plenty of books to read. David Adler's favorite books were mysteries, biographies, and baseball stories. Little did he know that, one day, he would write these kinds of stories for other young people to read.

ADLER HAS BEEN A NEW YORK YANKEES FAN SINCE CHILDHOOD.
HE LOVES TO WATCH BASEBALL GAMES AT YANKEE STADIUM IN NEW YORK CITY.

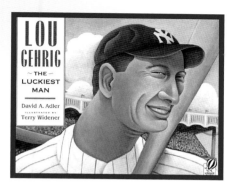

As a boy, David was a daydreamer and a storyteller. Some of his first stories were tall tales he created to entertain his brothers and sisters. In school, David enjoyed history and math classes most. After he graduated from college in 1968, he taught these two subjects in New York City schools.

One of Adler's first books for children was *A Little at a Time.* He got the idea for the book when his nephew kept asking him questions. Adler

---

ADLER SAYS HIS PARENTS, SIDNEY AND BETTY ADLER, ARE HIS ROLE MODELS.

A Selected Bibliography of Adler's Work

Fiction

The Babe & I (1999)

The Andy Russell Series (1998–2001) including:
    Andy Russell, NOT Wanted by the Police (2001)
    The Many Troubles of Andy Russell (1998)

Young Cam Jansen Series (1996–2006) including:
    Young Cam Jansen and the Double Beach Mystery (2002)
    Young Cam Jansen and the Missing Cookie (1996)
    Young Cam Jansen and the Spotted Cat Mystery (2006)

One Yellow Daffodil: A Hanukkah Story (1995)

The Cam Jansen Series (1980–2006) including:
    Cam Jansen and the Barking Treasure Mystery (2001)
    Cam Jansen and the Ghostly Mystery (1996)
    Cam Jansen and the Secret Service Mystery (2006)
    Cam Jansen and the Mystery of the Stolen Corn Popper (1986)
    Cam Jansen and the Mystery of the U.F.O. (1980)

A Little at a Time (1976)

Nonfiction

Satchel Paige: Don't Look Back (2007)

Campy: The Roy Campanella Story (2006)

Enemies of Slavery (2004)

Heroes of the Revolution (2003)

B. Franklin, Printer (2001)

America's Champion Swimmer: Gertrude Ederle (2000)

Shape Up! (1998)

Lou Gehrig: The Luckiest Man (1997)

Hilde and Eli, Children of the Holocaust (1994)

Picture Book Biography Series (1989–2001) including:
    A Picture Book of Jesse Owens (1996)
    A Picture Book of Eleanor Roosevelt (1991)
    A Picture Book of Martin Luther King, Jr. (1989)

The Number on My Grandfather's Arm (1987)

Our Golda, The Story of Golda Meir (1984)

3D, 2D, 1D (1975)

Base Five (1975)

Adler's Major Literary Awards

2001 Orbis Pictus Honor Book
    America's Champion Swimmer: Gertrude Ederle

1997 Boston Globe–Horn Book Nonfiction Honor Book
    Lou Gehrig: The Luckiest Man

1985 Carter G. Woodson Outstanding Merit Book
    Our Golda, The Story of Golda Meir

sent his book to a publisher and forgot about it. Months later, he was surprised and thrilled when the book was accepted. He continued teaching math until 1977. Then he decided he wanted to write all the time.

Adler writes both nonfiction and fiction. He especially likes writing biographies of famous people. Adler picks people that fascinate him. One of his favorite subjects to research and write about was Lou Gehrig—a record-breaking first baseman for the New York Yankees. Adler has also written about Helen Keller, Martin Luther King Jr., Anne Frank, and Jackie Robinson.

Adler has a unique way of finding information about people who lived long ago. He looks for encyclopedias that were written when that person was alive. To get a feel for what his subject's life was like, Adler uses the encyclopedias to study the places where the person lived. He also looks at newspapers from that person's time. Finally, Adler uses plenty of quotes from his subject. He believes that the voice of the subject should pop off the page and tell the story of that person's life.

"My greatest pleasure as a writer comes when I watch one of my children enjoying something I have written."

When he's working on fiction, Adler goes with what he knows. He often bases his characters on people he knows and likes. Cam Jansen, a girl detective, was based on a friend Adler met in first grade. Cam has

ONE OF ADLER'S FAVORITE CHARACTERS IS ANDY RUSSELL.
ANDY IS BASED ON ONE OF ADLER'S THREE CHILDREN.

become so popular that some kids have created Web sites all about her!

Adler likes to write books that make kids think. His mysteries are filled with clues and are fun to solve. He also writes books filled with puzzles, riddles, and brain teasers. Although Adler has written dozens of books, his fans don't need to worry. This amazing author says he has many more tales to tell.

"Dreamers become writers, and for me, being a published writer is a dream come true."

WHERE TO FIND OUT MORE ABOUT DAVID A. ADLER

BOOKS

Adler, David. *My Writing Day.* Katonah, N.Y.: Richard C. Owen, 1999.

McElmeel, Sharron L. *100 Most Popular Children's Authors: Biographical Sketches and Bibliographies.* Englewood, Colo.: Libraries Unlimited, 1999.

WEB SITES

DAVID ADLER HOME PAGE
http://www.davidaadler.com/
For a list of his works, a biographical sketch and more

EDUCATIONAL PAPERBACK ASSOCIATION
http://edupaperback.org/showauth.cfm?authid=12
For an autobiographical sketch of David Adler, a selection of books, and awards

SCHOLASTIC AUTHORS ONLINE BIOGRAPHY: DAVID ADLER
http://www2.scholastic.com/teachers/authorsandbooks/authorstudies/authorhome.jhtml?authorID=1794&collateralID=6675&displayName=Biography
To read an autobiographical sketch, a booklist, and an interview

Arnold Adoff

Born: July 16, 1935

rnold Adoff grew up in a noisy home. "In order to hold status within the family," he recalls, "you had to speak loudly." Eventually, Adoff would find his loudest voice through poetry. He has published more than thirty anthologies, or collections, of poems. Some are by African American poets, and others are his own creations.

Arnold Adoff was born in New York City in 1935. His parents were Russian Jewish immigrants. They instilled in Arnold a respect for his Jewish heritage, as well as a deep concern for social justice. The Adoff family lived in New York's South Bronx neighborhood. It was a multicultural community, and Arnold grew up among people of many different backgrounds.

At home, there were always heated discussions about current issues.

———

ARNOLD'S GRANDMOTHER WOULD NOT ALLOW HIM TO READ COMIC BOOKS BECAUSE THEY WERE TOO "LOWBROW." SHE DIDN'T BELIEVE THAT THEY WERE ENOUGH OF AN INTELLECTUAL CHALLENGE FOR HER GRANDSON.

Music filled the household, too. Arnold's mother played the violin, and his aunt sang. The sounds of opera, gospel, and jazz music streamed from the radio. By the time Arnold was in high school, he was totally hooked on jazz.

> *"We all need someone to point out that the emperor is wearing no clothes. That's the poet's job."*

During high school, Arnold planned to become a doctor. But his heart wasn't in it, and he ended up majoring in history and literature at the City College of New York, graduating in 1956. He continued his studies at Columbia University (1956–58) and the New School for Social Research (1965–67). Adoff also became an active supporter of the civil rights movement, which was heating up in the 1950s.

During the late 1950s, Adoff was jazz musician Charles Mingus's manager. Through Mingus, he met African American writer Virginia Hamilton. She and Adoff married in 1960. Hamilton went on to become a well-known children's book author. They had two children together—daughter Leigh and son Jaime.

> *"Writing a poem is making music with words and space."*

The couple lived in Spain and France for a while after they were married. But they were ultimately drawn back to the United States, so they could be more active in the civil rights movement.

ADOFF'S FIRST BOOK OF HIS OWN POETRY, *MA nDA LA*, USES ONLY WORDS THAT CONTAIN THE SOUND "AH."

A Selected Bibliography of Adoff's Work

Original Works:

Daring Dog and Captain Cat (2001)

The Return of Rex and Ethel (2000)

Love Letters (1997)

Touch the Poem (1996)

Chocolate Dreams (1988)

All the Colors of the Race (1982)

Today We Are Brother and Sister (1981)

I Am the Running Girl (1979)

Black Is Brown Is Tan (1973)

MA nDA LA (1971)

Malcolm X (1970)

Anthologies of Others' Work:

Celebrations (1977)

My Black Me (1974)

The Poetry of Black America (1973)

Black Out Loud (1970)

City in All Directions (1969)

I Am the Darker Brother (1968)

For twelve years, Adoff taught school in New York City's Harlem and Upper West Side communities. Most of his students were African Americans. Yet Adoff couldn't help noticing that there was very little African American literature available in schools at that time. He was determined to change this. He gathered together a collection of poetry by African Americans, and this became his first published anthology—*I Am the Darker Brother*. He went on to compile many anthologies of African American poetry as well as collections of fiction and commentaries by black writers.

Adoff spent many nights soaking up the sounds in jazz clubs. This inspired him to shape his own poetry with lively rhythms, creating what he calls "singing poems." The first of Adoff's many books of original poetry appeared in 1971. Two later books, *Black Is Brown Is Tan* and *All the Colors of the Race*, portray life for children of mixed-race marriages. For these titles, Adoff drew on his experiences as the father of an interracial family.

Adoff enjoys visiting schools around the country. He reads his poems and teaches poetry and creative writing. Adoff currently lives in Yellow Springs, Ohio.

WHERE TO FIND OUT MORE ABOUT ARNOLD ADOFF

BOOKS

Berger, Laura Stanley, ed. *Twentieth-Century Young Adult Writers*. Detroit: St. James Press, 1994.

Pendergast, Sara, and Tom Pendergast, eds. *St. James Guide to Children's Writers*. 5th ed. Detroit: St. James Press, 1999.

WEB SITES

ARNOLD ADOFF
http://www.arnoldadoff.com/
For information about the author

FIND ARTICLES
http://www.findarticles.com/p/articles/mi_m2342/is_3_35/ai_97074160
To read an article about Arnold Adoff regarding adolescent voice

----

ADOFF'S WIFE, VIRGINIA HAMILTON, DIED OF CANCER IN 2002.

Allan Ahlberg
Janet Ahlberg

Born: June 5, 1938 (Allan)
Born: October 21, 1944 (Janet)   *Died: November 15, 1994 (Janet)*

eek-a-boo babies, giant bean stalks, scary forests, and hidden clues—they're all part of the whimsical world of Allan and Janet Ahlberg. This British husband-and-wife, author-and-illustrator team produced dozens of books over twenty years. They thought of themselves as bookmakers, weaving stories and designs into a fresh, inventive whole.

Janet Hall was born in Huddersfield, England, in 1944 and grew up in Leicester. She showed a great talent for art, and her parents encouraged her. Allan Ahlberg, meanwhile, was born in Croydon, England, in 1938 and grew up near Birmingham. Since childhood, he dreamed of being a writer. He had no clear idea of how to pursue that, though, and decided to work as a teacher. So did Janet. The two met at the Sunderland College of Education and married in 1969.

Allan taught elementary school for ten years. Janet, however, decided to concentrate on her art. After studying graphic design at

---

THE AHLBERGS' DAUGHTER, JESSICA, WAS BORN IN **1980**. HAVING A YOUNG CHILD AROUND WAS A GREAT INSPIRATION FOR HER PARENTS.

Leicester Polytechnic, she worked as a freelance designer and illustrator.

But Janet yearned for more creative outlets. One day, she asked Allan to write a children's book that she could illustrate. Allan recalls he felt like "a clockwork toy and she had turned the key." The Ahlbergs' first book—*Here Are the Brick Street Boys*—was published in 1975. Four more Brick Street Boys books would follow in this popular series.

Soon the couple settled into a method that led to even more literary success and that showed their incredible teamwork. First, Allan thought of a story and told Janet about it. She then made drawings to show him. Back and

A Selected Bibliography of Allan Ahlberg's Work

Runaway Dinner (Writing only, 2006)
Children Who Smelled a Rat (Writing only, 2005)
Shopping Expedition (Writing only, 2005)
Half a Pig (Writing only, 2004)
The Cat Who Got Carried Away (Writing only, 2003)
The Woman Who Won Things (Writing only, 2002)
Slow Dog Falling (Writing only, 1999)
The Black Cat (Writing only, 1990)
Miss Brick the Builder's Baby (Writing only, 1982)

A Selected Bibliography of the Ahlbergs' Work

The Jolly Pocket Postman (1995)
It Was a Dark and Stormy Night (1993)
The Bear Nobody Wanted (1992)
Bye-Bye, Baby (1989)
The Jolly Postman (1986)
The Baby's Catalogue (1982)
The Ha Ha Bonk Book (1982)
Peek-a-Boo! (1981)
Mr. Biff the Boxer (1980)
The Little Worm Book (1979)
Jeremiah in the Dark Woods (1977)
Each Peach Pear Plum: An "I Spy" Story (1978)
Burglar Bill (1977)
Here Are the Brick Street Boys (1975)

Ahlbergs' Major Literary Awards

1991 Kate Greenaway Medal
  The Jolly Christmas Postman
1978 Kate Greenaway Medal
  Each Peach Pear Plum: An "I Spy" Story

forth they went, time and again—responding to each other, sparking ideas, and building on the other's work.

At last, they had a finished product to present to a publisher. And the products they created were hits! *Peek-a-Boo!* has peepholes to look through. *The Jolly Postman* features envelopes with actual letters tucked inside. *The Jolly Pocket Postman* comes with a magnifying lens because "there's more in here than meets the eye." And in the Slot Books series, the reader can insert cutouts into different slots.

> *"The thing which does drive us on is an urge not to do the exact same thing again."*
> —Janet Ahlberg

Many of the Ahlbergs' books tell the stories of happy families in England's Midlands Region in the 1950s. Allan's plots are often odd—even absurd—yet they are full of warm and cozy feelings. And Janet's intricate illustrations are rich, and full of engrossing details.

> *"[I]t is vital to be aware of the book as a physical, bound object—that you hold, with pages that turn."*
> —Allan Ahlberg

Allan used to joke that it took him a day to write a book, but it took Janet six months to do the illustrations. That's a bit of an exaggeration, but Allan did have extra time to work with other

THE AHLBERGS' BOOKS HAVE BEEN TRANSLATED INTO TWENTY-THREE LANGUAGES, INCLUDING FINNISH, HEBREW, AND JAPANESE.

illustrators. Some books he did apart from Janet at that time include the Happy Families series and the Funnybones series, featuring skeletons that take off on silly adventures.

Janet died of cancer in 1994 at the age of fifty. Allan was filled with loss. For almost a year, he sat around by himself, not knowing quite what to do. Finally, he got back to work again. Among the books he came out with after Janet's death are the titles in the Fast Fox, Slow Dog series. Allan now makes his home in London.

❧

WHERE TO FIND OUT MORE ABOUT ALLAN AND JANET AHLBERG

BOOKS

McElmeel, Sharron L. *100 Most Popular Picture Book Authors and Illustrators: Biographical Sketches and Bibliographies*. Englewood, Colo.: Libraries Unlimited, 2000.

Silvey, Anita, ed. *The Essential Guide to Children's Books and Their Creators*. Boston: Houghton Mifflin Company, 2002.

Berger, Laura Standley, ed. *Twentieth-Century Children's Writers*. 4th ed. Detroit: St. James Press, 1995.

WEB SITES

EDINBURGH CITY LIBRARIES
http://www.edinburgh.gov.uk/CEC/Recreation/Libraries/Fine_Art_Library/Childrens_Illustrators/janetahlberg.html
To read about Janet's life, work, and relationship with Allan

JANET AND ALLAN AHLBERG
http://coe.west.asu.edu/students/dcorley/authors/Ahlberg.htm
To read about their work

——

BEFORE HE BECAME A WRITER, ALLAN WORKED AS A SCHOOLTEACHER, POSTMAN, GRAVE DIGGER, AND PLUMBER'S ASSISTANT.

Joan Aiken

Born: September 4, 1924
Died: January 4, 2004

In British history, George I became king when Queen Anne died in 1714. The supporters of James Stuart, believing he should be king, rebelled. In Joan Aiken's best-known books, however, history takes a wild detour. James Stuart becomes King James III, and George's supporters carry out bizarre and horrifying plots to regain the throne. At one point, St. Paul's Cathedral in London is rolled into the River Thames! Meanwhile, life in England is strange and hard. Wolves terrorize the countryside (having migrated from Europe through a tunnel dug under the English

Channel). And King Arthur, 1,300 years after his reign, is discovered to be alive and working as a sea captain.

Aiken's James III novels—beginning with *The Wolves of Willoughby Chase* and continuing with *Black Hearts in Battersea, Nightbirds on Nantucket,* and *The Stolen Lake*—are among her best-known books. Each contains striking elements of fantasy. But mystery and magic, spooks and

FOUR OF AIKEN'S BOOKS FOR ADULTS ARE CONTINUATIONS, OR SEQUELS, TO THE NOVELS OF JANE AUSTEN, THE GREAT ENGLISH NOVELIST WHO LIVED FROM 1775 TO 1817 AND WROTE *PRIDE AND PREJUDICE* AND *SENSE AND SENSIBILITY.*

26

suspense, are an important part of much of Aiken's work. And she has written more than sixty books for children and thirty for adults.

When she was five years old, Joan Aiken bought a notebook and decided she wanted to be a writer. That's probably no surprise—Joan Aiken grew up around writers. Her father was the famous American poet Conrad Aiken. After her parents divorced, Joan's mother married the English novelist Martin Armstrong. As she grew up, Joan made up stories to entertain her younger brother. She filled her notebook with descriptions of places (some of them said to be haunted) near her home in Sussex, England. Some of these stories and descriptions eventually found their way into her books.

> *"Older readers grow lazier, while younger readers are more adventurous and prepared to work harder. My grandchildren tackle books that I would not have the stamina to attempt, but our tastes still overlap."*

Joan Aiken was born on September 4, 1924, and her native England was in the grip of the Great Depression during much of her childhood. Her older siblings went to boarding school, but there wasn't enough money to send Joan. She was taught at home by her mother until she was twelve.

When Joan eventually arrived at boarding school, she found it noisy, ugly, and hard to bear. Worse yet, the school went bankrupt and had to merge with another, larger school. Joan was so upset that she got sick

---

AIKEN'S FIRST NOVEL, *THE KINGDOM AND THE CAVE*, WAS PUBLISHED WHEN SHE WAS THIRTY-SIX YEARS OLD. BUT SHE WROTE THE FIRST DRAFT OF THE STORY WHEN SHE WAS SEVENTEEN.

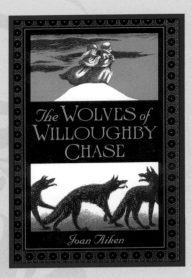

A Selected Bibliography of Aiken's Work

Witch of Clatteringshaws (2005)
Midwinter Nightingale (2003)
The Whispering Mountain (2002)
Shadows and Moonshine: Stories (2001)
Dangerous Games (1999)
Cold Shoulder Road (1996)
The Cockatrice Boys (1996)
A Creepy Company: Ten Tales of Terror (1995)
Is Underground (1993)
A Fit of Shivers: Tales for Late at Night (1992)
A Foot in the Grave (1991)
The Shoemaker's Boy (1991)
Return to Harken House (1990)
The Last Slice of Rainbow and Other Stories (1988)
The Teeth of the Gale (1988)
Mortimer Says Nothing (1985)
Up the Chimney Down and Other Stories (1984)
Bridle the Wind (1983)
Arabel and Mortimer (1981)
The Stolen Lake (1981)
Arabel's Raven (1974)
Night Fall (1970)
Nightbirds on Nantucket (1966)
Black Hearts in Battersea (1964)
The Wolves of Willoughby Chase (1963)

and missed most of a term. Her grades dropped, and she couldn't get into Oxford University as she had planned.

Instead, Joan Aiken went to work for the British Broadcasting Corporation (BBC), England's radio network, and then for the United Nations (UN) in London. While at the UN she met her future husband, Ron Brown. The UN job was a good one, but Aiken and her husband decided to leave London. Aiken and Brown moved to the countryside, not far from where Aiken had grown up. She worked on her writing, and her first book, *All You've Ever Wanted and Other Stories,* was published in England in 1953.

Aiken's husband died in 1955, and she had to support herself and her two children. She got a job as a magazine editor and continued to work on her stories. Her first novel, *The Kingdom and the Cave,* was published in England in 1960. Then came *The Wolves of Willoughby Chase,* which not only introduced readers to Aiken's private world, but also launched her career in the United States.

In 1975, Aiken was made a member of the Order of the British Empire for her services to children's literature. She lived in Sussex with her second husband, painter Julius Goldstein, until her death in 2004.

❧

WHERE TO FIND OUT MORE ABOUT JOAN AIKEN

BOOKS

Cullinan, Bernice E., and Diane G. Person, ed. *Continuum Encyclopedia of Children's Literature.* New York: Continuum, 2001.

Silvey, Anita, ed. *The Essential Guide to Children's Books and Their Creators.* Boston: Houghton Mifflin Company, 2002.

WEB SITES

MARSHALL UNIVERSITY
http://webpages.marshall.edu/~pbostic/author.html
To read a biography and bibliography

UNIVERSITY OF SOUTHERN MISSISSIPPI DE GRUMMOND COLLECTION
http://www.lib.usm.edu/%7Edegrum/html/research/findaids/aiken.htm
For a brief biographical sketch about Aiken, a selection of her works, and links to other related Web sites

⸻

FOR A WHILE AFTER WORLD WAR II (1939–1945), AIKEN LIVED WITH HER HUSBAND AND CHILDREN IN AN OLD BUS!

Louisa May Alcott

Born: November 29, 1832
Died: March 6, 1888

When she was only fifteen, Louisa May Alcott was already determined to become a success. "I will do something by and by," she claimed. "Don't care what . . . anything to help the family; and I'll be rich and famous and happy before I die, see if I won't!" Her prediction came true. Alcott went on to become one of America's most

beloved children's book authors. Her best-known classic is *Little Women*, featuring sisters Meg, Jo, Beth, and Amy.

Louisa was born in Germantown, Pennsylvania, in 1832. She had an older sister, Anna, and two younger sisters, Elizabeth and May. Louisa's mother, Abigail, was a social worker who believed in women's rights and opposed slavery. Her father, Amos Bronson Alcott, was a leader in the Transcendentalist movement. Transcendentalists believe that people can use their own minds to reach an ideal spiritual state.

TRANSCENDENTALIST WRITERS RALPH WALDO EMERSON AND HENRY DAVID THOREAU WERE FRIENDS OF THE ALCOTT FAMILY. ALCOTT ENJOYED EXPLORING EMERSON'S LIBRARY AND TAKING NATURE WALKS WITH THOREAU.

The Alcott family moved to Concord, Massachusetts, in 1840. There Louisa wrote plays that she and her sisters performed for friends. Louisa liked playing the shady characters—those she described as "the villains, ghosts, bandits, and disdainful queens." Louisa was a tomboy, too, just like her character Jo in *Little Women*.

In 1843, the Alcotts joined a community called the Fruitlands in Harvard, Massachusetts. Built on Transcendentalist principles, it was, according to Louisa, an experiment in "plain living and high thinking." Residents ate no animal products and used no animals for farm labor, and no one engaged in buying or selling. This was to

A Selected Bibliography of Alcott's Work
Jo's Boys (1886)
Spinning-Wheel Stories (1884)
Jack and Jill (1880)
Under the Lilacs (1878)
Rose in Bloom (1876)
Eight Cousins (1875)
Work (1873)
Aunt Jo's Scrap-Bag (Six volumes., 1872–1882)
Little Men (1871)
An Old-Fashioned Girl (1870)
Little Women (Two volumes, 1868–1869)
Moods (1865)
Hospital Sketches (1863)
Flower Fables (1855)

free their bodies and minds for spiritual pursuits. The community failed, however, and the Alcotts returned to Concord after only a few months. Soon they moved to Boston, Massachusetts.

Louisa was frustrated by the family's poverty. To help support them, she taught, worked as a seamstress, and did other people's laundry.

Determined to make more money, Alcott launched her writing career. Her first published work was the poem "Sunlight." It appeared in *Peterson's Magazine* in 1852. Her first book, *Flower Fables*, was published in 1855. During the Civil War (1861–1865), Alcott worked part of the time as a nurse in an army hospital in Washington, D.C. She wrote about her experiences in *Hospital Sketches*.

After the war, Alcott's publisher urged her to write a "girls' story." In less than three months, she produced *Little Women*, based on the four girls in her own family. Published in 1868, it was an instant success. A second *Little Women* volume came out the following year. Alcott welcomed the financial security that came with her success. She wrote in her journal, "Paid up all the debts . . . thank the Lord!"

Alcott continued to publish popular books, living sometimes in Boston and sometimes in Concord. She took

> *"My wise mother, anxious to give me a strong body to support a lively brain, turned me loose in the country and let me run wild, learning of Nature what no books can teach."*

WHILE WORKING AS A NURSE, ALCOTT CAUGHT TYPHOID FEVER AND WAS GIVEN CALOMEL, A DRUG THAT CONTAINED MERCURY. SHE SUFFERED FROM THE EFFECTS OF MERCURY POISONING FOR THE REST OF HER LIFE.

time to care for her ailing mother, who died in 1877. Other tragedies followed. Alcott's youngest sister, May, had a baby girl in 1879 and named her Louisa May (nicknamed Lulu). Sadly, May died a few weeks after Lulu's birth. According to May's wishes, Alcott took Lulu in and raised her. In 1885, Alcott moved into an elegant house in Boston, where she cared for both her aging father and Lulu. On March 4, 1888, her father passed away. Alcott died just two days later, at the age of fifty-five.

> *"I plod away [on* Little Women*], though I don't enjoy this sort of thing. Never liked girls or knew many, other than my sisters; but our queer plays and experiences might be interesting, though I doubt it."*

WHERE TO FIND OUT MORE ABOUT LOUISA MAY ALCOTT

BOOKS

Eiselein, Gregory, and Anne K. Phillips, eds. *The Louisa May Alcott Encyclopedia.* Westport, Conn.: Greenwood, 2002.

Gormley, Beatrice. *Louisa May Alcott: Young Novelist* (Childhood of Famous Americans Series). New York: Simon & Schuster Children's, 1999.

Silverthorne, Elizabeth. *Louisa May Alcott.* Philadelphia: Chelsea House, 2002.

WEB SITES

ABOUT THE AUTHOR
http://xroads.virginia.edu/~hyper/ALCOTT/ABOUTLA.html
For a biography of Louisa May Alcott

LITTLE WOMEN
http://xroads.virginia.edu/~HYPER/ALCOTT/LWHP.html
To view a hypermedia presentation about the author

Lloyd Alexander

Born: January 30, 1924

Although his parents thought it was a terrible idea, Lloyd Alexander knew when he was fifteen years old that he wanted to be a writer. Alexander has been writing for more than fifty years and has published more than fifty books for children and adults.

Lloyd Chudley Alexander was born on January 30, 1924, in Philadelphia, Pennsylvania. He learned how to read when he was just three years

old. He always enjoyed reading and especially liked Greek and Celtic mythology as a child.

Alexander attended college for a short time and then dropped out. He was disappointed that the courses did not seem to prepare him to be a writer. He joined the U.S. Army and was sent to Europe during World War II (1939–1945). After the war, he attended the University of Paris. There, he met—and married—a young woman

BEFORE HE BECAME A PUBLISHED WRITER, ALEXANDER WORKED AS A CARTOONIST, ADVERTISING WRITER, LAYOUT ARTIST, AND EDITOR OF A SMALL MAGAZINE.

named Janine Denni. Alexander enjoyed Europe, but knew "if I was going to write anything worthwhile, I would have to be closer to my own roots."

So Alexander returned to Drexel Hill, Pennsylvania, and began his career as a writer. He wrote for seven years before his first book was published—a book written for adults. It was more than ten years before he began writing for young people.

Most of Alexander's books have a fantasy theme. His love for writing fantasy started as a child. "I loved all the world's mythologies," Alexander notes. "King Arthur was one of my heroes." Alexander believes he is best able to express his true feelings and relationships through writing fantasy.

Alexander also loves writing for children. He learned early on that he was able to be more creative when writing for young people.

Along with fantasy, Alexander includes humor in his books. He believes that readers need a break from serious writing. The humor allows his readers to smile and laugh while still enjoying the story.

For Alexander, writing is a very difficult process. He begins by reading and doing research. Before he

> *"I never did find out all I wanted to know about writing and realize I never will. All that writers can do is to keep trying to say what is deepest in their hearts."*

> *"Fantasy is hardly an escape from reality. It's a way of understanding it."*

AFTER HIGH SCHOOL, ALEXANDER WORKED FOR A WHILE AS A MESSENGER BOY FOR A LOCAL BANK. HE SAYS THAT EXPERIENCE WAS MISERABLE!

A Selected Bibliography of Alexander's Work

Dream-of-Jade: the Emperor's Cat (2005)

Time Cat: The Remarkable Journeys of Jason and Gareth (2003)

The Fortune-Tellers (1992)

The Vesper Holly Adventures
The Philadelphia Adventure (1990)
The Drackenberg Adventure (1988)
The Illyrian Adventure (1986)

The Westmark Trilogy
The Beggar Queen (1984)
The Kestrel (1982)
Westmark (1981)

The Cat Who Wished to Be a Man (1973)

The Marvelous Misadventures of Sebastian (1970)

Miscellaneous Prydain Books
The Foundling and Other Tales of Prydain (1999)
The Truthful Harp (1967)
Coll and His White Pig (1965)

The Prydain Chronicles
The High King (1968)
Taran Wanderer (1967)
The Castle of Llyr (1966)
The Black Cauldron (1965)
The Book of Three (1964)

Alexander's Major Literary Awards

1993 Boston Globe–Horn Book Picture Book Award
The Fortune-Tellers

1982 American Book Award
Westmark

1973 Boston Globe–Horn Book Fiction Honor Book
The Cat Who Wished to Be a Man

1971 National Book Award
The Marvelous Misadventures of Sebastian

1969 Newbery Medal
The High King

1966 Newbery Honor Book
The Black Cauldron

begins writing a book, he takes notes and writes an outline. The process of rewriting is also difficult for Alexander. "Every writer except some great genius has to rewrite," Alexander explains. He has rewritten some pages up to thirty times and some chapters three or four times. He has even rewritten entire books.

For Alexander, reading is the most important part of becoming an author. He encourages children who want to be writers to read as much as they can. Writing every day and learning to enjoy writing are also important. Both reading and writing help to create a wonderful imagination.

Alexander still lives in Pennsylvania with his wife. He continues to write books for children.

✂

WHERE TO FIND OUT MORE ABOUT LLOYD ALEXANDER

BOOKS

May, Jill P. *Lloyd Alexander.* New York: Twayne, 1991.

McElmeel, Sharron L. *100 Most Popular Children's Authors: Biographical Sketches and Bibliographies.* Englewood, Colo.: Libraries Unlimited, 1999.

Wheeler, Jill C. *Lloyd Alexander.* Edina, Minn.: Abdo & Daughters, 1997.

WEB SITES

CBC MAGAZINE
http://www.cbcbooks.org/cbcmagazine/meet/lloydalexander.html
For an article written by the author

KIDSREADS.COM
http://www.kidsreads.com/authors/au-alexander-lloyd.asp
For a biography and list of works

SCHOLASTIC AUTHORS ONLINE BIOGRAPHY
http://books.scholastic.com/teachers/authorsandbooks/authorstudies/authorhome.
jsp?authorID=1&displayName=Biography
To read a biography and list of works

SOUND RECORDING
Lloyd Alexander, Born Story Teller: Edna Edwards Interviews the Noted Children's Author.
North Hollywood, Calif.: Center for Cassette Studies, 1973.

ALEXANDER GETS UP AT 3 OR 4 A.M. TO WORK ON HIS WRITING. WHEN HE HAS TROUBLE WITH HIS WRITING, HE GOES BACK TO BED. HIS WIFE SAYS HE GOES BACK TO SLEEP, BUT ALEXANDER CALLS IT "THINKING HORIZONTALLY."

Harry Allard

Born: January 27, 1928

If Harry Allard had not taught French at Trinity University in San Antonio, Texas, he never would have met James Marshall—one of his pupils. Marshall went on to become a children's author and illustrator best known for the George and Martha books. Harry Allard moved to New Haven, Connecticut, to attend Yale and work on his doctorate. There he met Marshall again. Marshall's art inspired Allard to create his first book, *The Stupids Step Out,* with Marshall. In it, the slow-witted Stanley Stupid, along with his wife, Mrs. Stupid, their children, Buster and Petunia, and their dog, Kitty, spend a day doing ridiculous things. The book was an instant hit with young readers.

Allard's next book was *Miss Nelson Is Missing!* The book tells how Miss Nelson teaches her unruly students a lesson. She pretends to be missing but dresses in a black dress and wig to become the mean substitute teacher—Viola Swamp. Miss Swamp is so mean that the children are grateful to have Miss Nelson back and begin to behave beautifully.

THE STUPIDS STEP OUT WAS INCLUDED ON THE *SCHOOL LIBRARY JOURNAL* "BEST OF THE BEST 1966–1978" LIST.

Whenever Allard and Marshall worked on a new book, the text came first. Usually, the first draft of a book came quickly to Allard. But he believed that revision was the key to a good book. As he revised, Allard worked to make sentences as simple as possible. He and Marshall worked closely. Allard suggested illustrations. As Marshall finished illustrations, Allard revised the words, taking out anything that was in Marshall's drawing. Allard and Marshall worked together until Marshall's death in 1992. Since then, a few of Allard's books have been illustrated by other artists.

Allard's books do not have moral messages for children.

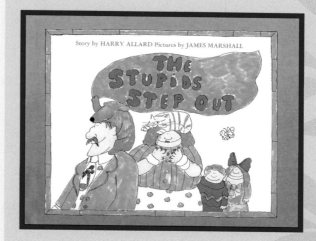

A Selected Bibliography of Allard's Work

The Cactus Flower Bakery (1991)
Hummingbird's Day (1991)
The Stupids Take Off (1989)
Miss Nelson Has a Field Day (1985)
Miss Nelson Is Back (1982)
The Stupids Die (1981)
There's a Party at Mona's Tonight (1981)
Three Is Company (1980)
Bumps in the Night (1979)
I Will Not Go to Market Today (1979)
May I Stay? (1978)
The Stupids Have a Ball (1978)
Crash Helmet (1977)
It's So Nice to Have a Wolf around the House (1977)
Miss Nelson Is Missing! (1977)
The Tutti-Frutti Case: Starring the Four Doctors of Goodge (1975)
The Stupids Step Out (1974)

They do not try to teach them to love others or respect the elderly or behave properly in school. Allard thinks there are too many "message" books. His books simply tell wild and wonderfully funny stories. His personal favorite is *It's So Nice to Have a Wolf around the House*.

Three of Allard's titles—*It's So Nice to Have a Wolf around the House, Miss Nelson Is Missing!* and *Miss Nelson Is Back*—have been turned into motion pictures or television programs. Several of his books have won major awards. *The Tutti-Frutti Case: Starring the Four Doctors of Goodge* was named a *New York Times* Best Illustrated Children's Book of the Year in 1975. *I Will Not Go to Market Today* was exhibited in the 1980 American Institute of Graphic Arts show. James Marshall illustrated both books. *Miss Nelson Is Missing!* was a runner-up for the Edgar Allan Poe Award from Mystery Writers of America.

Harry Allard didn't start out as a writer of children's books. He was born in Evanston, Illinois, on January 27, 1928, the birthday of Lewis Carroll, the creator of *Alice in Wonderland*. Allard graduated from

> The Stupids are popular because "children are always under the thumb of somebody—adults, whether they are parents or priests or nuns or whatever—and here the children can make fun of adults and feel superior to them and know more than they do."

THE STUPID SERIES RANKED TWENTY-SIXTH AMONG THE ONE HUNDRED BOOKS MOST OFTEN BANNED FROM LIBRARIES BETWEEN 1990 AND 2000. SOME ADULTS APPARENTLY FELT THAT THE SERIES MAKES FUN OF MENTALLY CHALLENGED PEOPLE.

Northwestern University in 1948 and
served in the U.S. Army in Korea.

Allard lived for three years in Paris
and then returned to the United States
to earn a Ph.D. in French. He taught
college-level French for many years and is now retired from Salem State
College. He lives in Oaxaca, Mexio.

"I now look upon sharing a birthday with the creator of Alice in Wonderland as a good omen."

❧

WHERE TO FIND OUT MORE ABOUT HARRY ALLARD

BOOKS
Berger, Laura Standley, ed. *Twentieth-Century Children's Writers.* 4th ed.
Detroit: St. James Press, 1995.

Collier, Laurie, and Joyce Nakamura eds. *Major Authors and Illustrators for Children and Young Adults: A Selection of Sketches from Something about the Author.*
Detroit: Gale Research, 1993.

Norby, Shirley, and Gregory Ryan. *Famous Children's Authors.*
Minneapolis: Denison, 1988.

WEB SITES
CHILDREN'S LITERATURE NETWORK
http://www.childrensliteraturenetwork.org/brthpage/01jan/1-27allard.html
To read a short biography

———

IN *THE STUPIDS DIE,* THE ELECTRICITY GOES OUT ONE NIGHT AFTER THE FAMILY
HAS GONE TO BED. THEY THINK THEY HAVE DIED. THE DOG AND CAT CHANGE THE
FUSE AND RESTORE POWER. THEN THE STUPIDS THINK THEY ARE IN HEAVEN.

M. T. Anderson

Born: November 4, 1968

Truth may be stranger than fiction, but M. T. Anderson's blend of reality and fantasy can be downright disturbing. Anderson is best known for his young-adult novels. His characters seem like ordinary, everyday teenagers—until they enter scary worlds where they wrestle with earth-shattering, life-threatening issues.

Matthew Tobin Anderson was born in Cambridge, Massachusetts, in 1968. His father is an engineer, and his mother is a priest in the

Episcopal Church. Although his books identify him as M. T., people usually call him Tobin.

"I always wanted to be a writer," he recalls. "Even as a little kid, I wrote little stories and things that I thought of as novels." As a teenager, Tobin began submitting stories to publishers. "At least it got me used to the series of rejections that come along with a writer's life," he confessed. Tobin also worked at a McDonald's restaurant when he

---

ANDERSON ENJOYS CLASSICAL MUSIC. HE HAS WRITTEN MUSIC REVIEWS FOR THE MAGAZINE *BBC MUSIC* AND HAS SUNG IN OPERA CHORUSES.

was a teenager. Little did he know that this experience would come in handy later in his career.

Anderson studied English literature at Harvard University in Cambridge, Massachusetts, in 1987 and received a degree from Cambridge University in England in 1991. After college, he got a job as an intern at Candlewick Press, a publisher in his hometown. Anderson continued to work there as an editorial assistant from 1993 to 1996. His job mainly involved making photocopies and assembling mailing lists.

Meanwhile, though, Anderson was working on a novel called *Thirsty*. It was a creepy tale about a high-school freshman in a small New England town who realizes he's turning into a vampire. When Anderson finally showed the story to his boss, she gently suggested that it needed a plot. After much revision, *Thirsty* was published in 1997, and Anderson's writing career was off and running.

"I go up to Maine occasionally and just get away from people, away from all of the discussion . . . and there, amidst the silence, I often find focus again. Suddenly, I am hearing the rhythms of my character again."

"I would say that there are two [themes] that recur [in my work]: One is the idea of how one remains moral in a world where you must consume or be consumed, and the other is the terrifying passage of time. I would say that those are the two main themes that I helplessly find myself repeating."

ANDERSON'S SHORT STORIES FOR YOUNG ADULTS HAVE APPEARED IN SEVERAL MAGAZINES AND SHORT-STORY COLLECTIONS.

A Selected Bibliography of Anderson's Work

Octavian Nothing (2007)
The Clue of the Linoleum Lederhosen (2006)
Me, All Alone, at the End of the World (2005)
The Serpent Came to Gloucester (2005)
Whales on Stilts! (2005)
The Game of Sunken Places (2004)
Strange Mr. Satie (2003)
Feed (2002)
Handel, Who Knew What He Liked (2001)
Burger Wuss (1999)
Thirsty (1997)

Anderson's Major Literary Awards

2003 Boston Globe-Horn Book Fiction Honor Book
  Feed
2002 Boston Globe-Horn Book Nonfiction Honor Book
  Handel, Who Knew What He Liked

Anderson's stint at McDonald's provided him with the background for his next novel, *Burger Wuss*. This tale of betrayal and revenge is centered on two teens who work at a hamburger joint.

Anderson's novel *Feed* is science fiction, but it comes frighteningly close to the realities of modern life. It takes place in a world where people are connected to a network through an electronic feed implanted in their brains. Through the feed, they receive education, entertainment, advertisements, and even contact with their friends. For Anderson, *Feed* raises questions about the way advertising and the Internet control our lives.

Anderson has also written several picture books for children, including biographies of composers George Frideric Handel and Erik Satie. Anderson chose these two because "they were people whose lives and struggles I felt would appeal to children." For example, Handel worried that people were making fun of him, and Satie threw tantrums and hated following rules.

In between writing projects, Anderson still manages to find time to study and teach. He obtained a degree in creative writing from Syracuse University in New York State in 1998. From 2000 to 2005, he taught writing at Vermont College in Montpelier, Vermont. Anderson currently lives in Cambridge, Massachusetts.

❧

WHERE TO FIND OUT MORE ABOUT M. T. ANDERSON

BOOKS

Rockman, Connie C., ed. *The Ninth Book of Junior Authors and Illustrators.*
New York: H. W. Wilson Company, 2004.

WEB SITES

BOOKPAGE
http://www.bookpage.com/0407bp/mt_anderson.html
To read an article and interview with M. T. Anderson

CANDLEWICK PRESS
http://www.candlewick.com/authill.asp?b=author&m=bio&id=2150&pix=n
To read a biography of M. T. Anderson

————

A GIANT SEA SERPENT WAS SIGHTED OFF THE COAST OF GLOUCESTER, MASSACHUSETTS, IN 1817. THAT'S THE SUBJECT OF ANDERSON'S RHYMING STORY *THE SERPENT CAME TO GLOUCESTER.*

William Armstrong

Born: September 14, 1914
Died: April 11, 1999

William Armstrong always thought of himself as a teacher rather than a writer. He taught high-school history for more than fifty years. He also wrote more than a dozen books, some for young people and some for adults. His novel *Sounder* has become a modern classic.

William Howard Armstrong was born in a village near Lexington, Virginia, in 1914. He and his two older sisters grew up in a hardworking, close-knit farming community. William's father ran the family farm, and his mother read the children Bible stories every day.

William helped out with the farm chores and cared for his beloved pet, a spotted pony. Working for five cents an hour, he dug pesky sassafras shoots out of a pasture. This job helped him earn money to buy his first book, a biography of Abraham Lincoln, for $1.65.

William's school life was fairly miserable. Other kids made fun of him because he was short, wore glasses, and had asthma. After William's pony

SOUNDER WAS TRANSLATED INTO TWENTY-EIGHT LANGUAGES.
IT ALSO WAS MADE INTO THE 1972 MOVIE *SOUNDER*, WHICH RECEIVED
FOUR ACADEMY AWARD NOMINATIONS.

died, he began to stutter. That brought on more ridicule from his schoolmates. Fortunately, William finally gained some self-confidence in sixth grade. His teacher held up a paper he had written and declared it to be the most neatly written paper in the class. At last, William realized he could succeed at something.

Another influence on William's life was an elderly, African American man who taught school and sometimes worked on the Armstrongs' farm. In the evenings, as the children sat around the kitchen table, he would tell wonderful stories. One night, he told a tale from his own life about a black family and their faithful coon dog, Sounder. William would hold

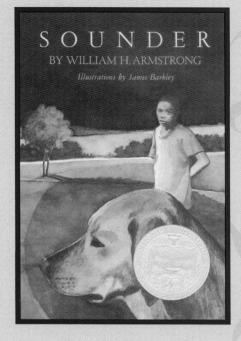

A Selected Bibliography of Armstrong's Work

Study Tactics (1983)
The Tale of Tawny and Dingo (1979)
Joanna's Miracle (1977)
Study Tips: How to Study Effectively and Get Better Grades (1975)
The Education of Abraham Lincoln (1974)
My Animals (1974)
The Mills of God (1973)
Hadassah: Esther the Orphan Queen (1972)
The MacLeod Place (1972)
Sour Land (1971)
Animal Tales (1970)
Barefoot in the Grass: The Story of Grandma Moses (1970)
Sounder (1969)
87 Ways to Help Your Child in School (1961)
Through Troubled Waters (1957)
Study Is Hard Work (1956)

Armstrong's Major Literary Award

1970 Newbery Medal
  Sounder

> *"[M]ost of my books begin with an idea that I take inside and keep there for a long time before I write a single word. It gets into my blood and is filtered through my heart until it is a part of me."*

the memory of this story in his heart for decades.

William attended high school at Augusta Military Academy in Fort Defiance, Virginia. In 1936, he graduated with honors from Hampden-Sydney College in Virginia. He married Martha Stone Street Williams in 1943.

Two years later, the couple moved to Kent, Connecticut, where Armstrong began teaching ninth grade at Kent School. In his free time, Armstrong cleared the rocks from a hillside overlooking the Housatonic River and built a pine house with his own hands. He and Martha lived there with their three children—Christopher, David, and Mary.

During Armstrong's time at Kent School, the headmaster encouraged him to write a book about good study habits. That effort resulted in his first published book, *Study Is Hard Work*, in 1956. Before he finished it, though, a tragic event occurred. Martha died suddenly in 1953. In *Through Troubled Waters*, Armstrong wrote about how he and the children struggled with her death.

IN HIGH SCHOOL, WILLIAM WROTE A SHORT STORY FOR A COMPOSITION CLASS. IT WAS SO GOOD THAT HIS TEACHERS THOUGHT HE HAD COPIED IT FROM ANOTHER AUTHOR.

But it was *Sounder* that gained Armstrong his greatest recognition. Reaching into his childhood memories, he brought to life the story he had heard from his old friend who had worked on the family farm. *Sounder*, published in 1969, was a wrenching tale of racial injustice, loyalty, and love. Armstrong's story was so long that he broke it into three separate books—*Sounder*, *Sour Land*, and *The MacLeod Place*.

More books would follow over the years. Armstrong went on to write biographies and more fictional works and study aids. He died in 1999 at the age of eighty-four.

"Early in the morning is my time to write—from 4:00 A.M. to 7:00 A.M. There is something very satisfactory about having one big job done before breakfast—like back on the farm with the milking before breakfast."

❧

WHERE TO FIND OUT MORE ABOUT WILLIAM ARMSTRONG

BOOKS

Beacham's Guide to Literature for Young Adults. Vol. 3. Osprey, Fla.: Beacham Publishing, 1990.

Chevalier, Tracy, ed. *Twentieth-Century Children's Writers.* 3rd ed. Detroit: St. James Press, 1989.

WEB SITES

CHILDREN'S LITERATURE NETWORK
http://www.childrensliteraturenetwork.org/brthpage/09sep/9-14armstrng.html
For a biography of the author

FROM 1939 TO 1944, ARMSTRONG TAUGHT AT VIRGINIA EPISCOPAL SCHOOL IN LYNCHBURG, VIRGINIA.

José Aruego

Born: August 9, 1932

No wonder José Aruego loves drawing animals. He grew up around dogs, cats, horses, chickens, frogs, ducks, and pigs. Now his comic animals frolic across the pages of more than sixty picture books. He wrote many of those books, too.

José Espiritu Aruego was born in Manila in the Philippines in 1932. As a child, he liked reading comic books and drawing pictures. Lots of pet animals lived in and around the family home, and José's sketches were usually of cartoon animals with funny personalities. José's father was a lawyer, and so were many of the Aruegos' family friends. José's older sister went to law school, and he was expected to follow the same career path. So he enrolled in the University of the Philippines, where he received his law degree in 1955.

It soon became clear, however, that Aruego was not destined to be a lawyer. He practiced law for only three months. In that time, he tried just one case, and he lost. Aruego knew he had to pursue his true love—art.

ARUEGO CREATED A MURAL, OR LARGE WALL PAINTING, AT NEW YORK CITY'S INTERNATIONAL HOUSE, A RESIDENTIAL COMMUNITY FOR FOREIGN STUDENTS.

He moved to New York City, where he enrolled in Parsons School of Design. In 1959, he received a certificate in graphic arts and advertising.

> *"Each project teaches me something new and makes me a better artist. Each book brings me closer to children."*

After art school, Aruego worked as an apprentice in a New York art studio. At about this time, he met artist Ariane Dewey, and they married in 1961. For the next few years, Aruego held drawing and design jobs with various advertising agencies, design studios, and magazines. In his spare time, he drew cartoons. He was thrilled that some magazines accepted his work. In the mid-1960s, once he realized that he could sell his cartoons, he became a full-time cartoonist. His work appeared in magazines such as the *New Yorke*r and the *Saturday Evening Post*.

> *"Most of the characters in my books are animals. It seems no matter how I draw them they look funny."*

By 1968, Aruego was certain that he was mostly interested in writing and illustrating children's books—which he wanted to be filled with funny animals! His first book, *The King and His Friends*, was published in 1969. Next, he illustrated *Whose Mouse Are You?* by Robert Kraus. Aruego and Kraus realized they made an excellent team and have collaborated on several other books over the years. Many of these are stories about mice.

———
ARUEGO AND ARIANE DEWEY HAD ONE CHILD TOGETHER—A SON NAMED JUAN.

A Selected Bibliography of Aruego's Work

Last Laugh (2006)

Duck, Duck, Goose! A Coyote's on the Loose! (Illustrations only, 2004)

Splash! (2001)

How Chipmunk Got His Stripes (Illustrations only, 2001)

Mouse in Love (Illustrations only, 2000)

Safe, Warm, and Snug (Illustrations only, 1999)

Lizard's Home (Illustrations only, 1999)

Little Louie the Baby Bloomer (Illustrations only, 1998)

Antarctic Antics (Illustrations only, 1998)

They Thought They Saw Him (Illustrations only, 1996)

April Showers (Illustrations only, 1995)

Alligators and Others All Year Long (Illustrations only, 1993)

Merry-Go-Round (Illustrations only, 1992)

Birthday Rhymes, Special Times (1991)

Rockabye Crocodile: A Folktale from the Philippines (1988)

Lizard Song (Illustrations only, 1981)

Musical Max (Illustrations only, 1979)

We Hide, You Seek (1979)

Two Greedy Bears (1976)

Herman the Helper (1974)

A Crocodile's Tale (1972)

Leo the Late Bloomer (Illustrations only, 1971)

Whose Mouse Are You? (Illustrations only, 1970)

The King and His Friends (1969)

Aruego's Major Literary Award

1974 Boston Globe–Horn Book Picture Book Honor Book
  Herman the Helper

In creating his illustrations, Aruego often works with his wife, Ariane. Even though they divorced in 1973, they have continued illustrating together. Aruego, who likes drawing, designs the pages and sketches the outlines. Then Ariane, who likes painting, adds the color. One of their best-loved books is *We Hide, You Seek*. It features a clumsy rhinoceros stomping wildly through a jungle full of other animals.

Aruego continues to play different roles in the children's book industry. For some titles, he is both the writer and illustrator. Most of his books, however, are written by other people and illustrated by him and Ariane.

Whether he's drawing penguins, mice, alligators, or frogs, Aruego's characters are lovable, funny, and unforgettable. He continues to create them in his home studio in New York City.

WHERE TO FIND OUT MORE ABOUT JOSÉ ARUEGO

BOOKS

Children's Literature Review. Vol. 3. Detroit: Gale, 1983.

Fourth Book of Junior Authors & Illustrators. New York: H. W. Wilson Company, 1978.

Silvey, Anita, ed. *The Essential Guide to Children's Books and Their Creators.* Boston: Houghton Mifflin Company, 2002.

WEB SITES

HARPERCOLLINS
http://www.harperchildrens.com/teacher/catalog/author_xml.asp?authorID=11745&role=2
To read a biography of José Aruego

MEET THE ILLUSTRATOR
http://www.eduplace.com/kids/hmr/mtai/aruego_dewey.html
For a short biography about José and his painting partner Ariane Dewey

ARUEGO'S ANIMAL DRAWINGS ARE SO FUNNY THAT HE SOMETIMES FINDS HIMSELF GIGGLING AS HE CREATES THEM.

Avi

Born: December 23, 1937

Who is Avi? Where did that name come from? Both questions are frequently asked by children when they see that name on popular children's books. Avi is a well-known author. His name is actually a nickname! His twin sister, Emily, started calling him that when they were small children.

When Avi first started writing, he wrote plays. He began writing

children's books when his two sons were young. They played a game in which Avi told them stories. Soon, he began writing down these stories. Avi then discovered how much he enjoyed writing for children. He could write about anything, and he was also very good at it. Avi's first book was published in 1970. His children's books have won many awards.

Avi was born on December 23, 1937, in New York City. He grew up in Brooklyn, New York. Avi

IT TAKES AVI ABOUT A YEAR TO WRITE ONE OF HIS BOOKS.
HE NEEDS ABSOLUTE QUIET WHEN HE WRITES!

did not like to write when he was a child. It was very hard for him. But he always loved to read. Reading was important in his family. He read all kinds of books, including picture books, chapter books, comics, and magazines. He has said that reading is the key to writing.

Avi has often spoken about how difficult it was for him to learn to write. He had a learning disability called dysgraphia. Dysgraphia is the partial or whole inablility to form letters. Avi worked hard to overcome this problem.

When he is not writing, Avi spends a lot of time visiting schools. He likes to talk to students who are struggling with friends, with learning,

A Selected Bibliography of Avi's Work

Poppy's Return (2005)
Never Mind!: A Twin Novel (2004)
Mayor of Central Park (2003)
Crispin: The Cross of Lead (2002)
Silent Movie (2002)
Don't You Know There's a War On? (2001)
The Good Dog (2001)
The Christmas Rat (2000)
Midnight Magic (1999)
Finding Providence: The Story of Roger Williams (1997)
Poppy (1995)
The Barn (1994)
City of Light, City of Dark: A Comic Book Novel (1993)
Who Was That Masked Man, Anyway? (1992)
The True Confessions of Charlotte Doyle (1990)
Shadrach's Crossing: A Novel (1983)
Sometimes I Think I Hear My Name: A Novel (1982)
The Man from the Sky (1980)
Emily Upham's Revenge: A Massachusetts Adventure (1978)
Snail Tale: The Adventures of a Rather Small Snail (1972)
Things That Sometimes Happen (1970)

Avi's Major Literary Awards

2003 Newbery Medal
  Crispin: The Cross of Lead

1996 Boston Globe–Horn Book Fiction Award
  Poppy

1992 Boston Globe–Horn Book Fiction Honor Book
1992 Newbery Honor Book
  Nothing but the Truth: A Documentary Novel

1991 Boston Globe–Horn Book Fiction Award
1991 Newbery Honor Book
  The True Confessions of Charlotte Doyle

1985 Scott O'Dell Award
  The Fighting Ground

or with school. He shows them samples of his writing that have been edited for various errors. He shows them how even an award-winning author needs to work hard at being a better writer.

"I want my readers to feel, to think, sometimes to laugh. But most of all I want them to enjoy a good read."

Avi's stories begin slowly as he thinks about them. The story line doesn't just come to him from start to finish. It develops as Avi works on it and considers many things. First, he has an idea. Then, he looks at people. He also thinks about events and experiences. All these things come together over time to create the story.

Some of Avi's books are historical fiction. These books are made-up stories, but they are set during a real period in history. Avi believes it is very important for children to learn history. A knowledge

"I believe reading is the key to writing. The more you read, the better your writing can be."

of history helps us understand what is happening in the world today and what will happen in the future.

Avi has written other kinds of books, too. One—*City of Light, City of Dark: A Comic Book Novel*—is told completely in comic-strip panels! Some of his books are

IT IS OBVIOUS THAT AVI HAS A LOVE OF BOOKS. IN ADDITION TO READING AND WRITING BOOKS, HE WORKED AS A LIBRARIAN FOR TWENTY-FIVE YEARS!

for young readers and others are meant for older readers. But all his books have one thing in common—his readers love them.

⚘

WHERE TO FIND OUT MORE ABOUT AVI

BOOKS

Bloom, Susan P. *Presenting Avi.*
New York: Twayne Publishers, 1997.

Markham, Lois. *Avi.*
Santa Barbara, Calif.: Learning Works, 1996.

McElmeel, Sharron L. *100 Most Popular Children's Authors: Biographical Sketches and Bibliographies.* Englewood, Colo.: Libraries Unlimited, 1999.

WEB SITES

AVI HOME PAGE
http://www.avi-writer.com/
For a biography, a list of books, and a bulletin board

EDUCATIONAL PAPERBACK ASSOCIATION
http://edupaperback.org/showauth.cfm?authid=46
To read an autobiographical account by Avi and a selection
of his works, and to find out about his awards

INTERNET PUBLIC LIBRARY KID SPACE
http://www.ipl.org/div/kidspace/askauthor/Avi.html
For a short biography and FAQ's about the author

LEARNING ABOUT AVI
http://www.scils.rutgers.edu/~kvander/avi.html
To read a biographical account of Avi and
opinions on what makes his writing appealing to kids

───

PHOTOGRAPHY IS ONE OF AVI'S HOBBIES.

Mary Azarian

Born: December 8, 1940

Moonlit snowdrifts, barnyard animals, scenes of rural farming life—these are some of Mary Azarian's favorite subjects for her artwork. Using stark lines and rich colors, she has illustrated more than forty books.

This beloved artist was born Mary Schneider in 1940 in Washington, D.C. She grew up on the family's farm in northern Virginia. When she was just a girl, Mary started experimenting with woodcuts, or pictures printed from carved blocks of wood. She was interested in science, too. When she entered Smith College in Northampton, Massachusetts, she planned to major in medicine. Out of curiosity, she took some classes in printmaking and etching (carving designs onto metal or wood). She liked these classes so much that she switched her major to art.

AZARIAN'S WOODCUTS APPEAR ON NOTE CARDS AND CALENDARS AS WELL AS IN BOOKS.

> "After almost forty years of growing all manner of plants, I have almost learned how to garden."

In 1963, she graduated from Smith and married musician Tomas Azarian. The couple settled down on a farm in northern Vermont. There they grew vegetables and made maple syrup. They also raised horses, oxen, cows, chickens, and sheep—and three sons.

The year she moved to the farm, Azarian took a job teaching grades one through eight in a one-room schoolhouse in Walden, Vermont. She felt that the schoolroom walls looked awfully cold and bare. So Azarian made posters and hung them around the room. For each poster, she painted a letter of the alphabet and a picture of something starting with that letter.

In 1967, as her family grew, Azarian quit teaching so she could work at home. She started Farmhouse Press in 1969 to print her woodcut illustrations. She is still using this time-consuming technique today.

First, Azarian draws a picture onto a block of wood. Using Japanese woodcutting tools, she cuts away the background area, leaving the picture's outline. Next, she rolls ink over the design. She puts the inked block into her nineteenth-century, hand-operated press. Then

> "It's hard for kids to know what they really want to do. But if there's something they really, really want to do, they should try it even if it doesn't seem practical."

AZARIAN HAS THREE CATS—PHOEBE, TREY, AND BIG KITTY—AND A BEAGLE NAMED HILDA.

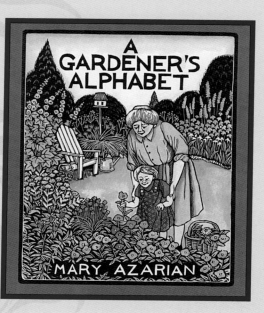

A Selected Bibliography of Azarian's Work

Spring (2006)

Unsigned Valentine (Illustrations only, 2006)

Miss Bridie Chose a Shovel (Illustrations only, 2004)

From Dawn till Dusk (Illustrations only, 2002)

When the Moon Is Full (Illustrations only, 2001)

The Race of the Birkebeiners (Illustrations only, 2001)

A Gardener's Alphabet (2000)

Snowflake Bentley (Illustrations only, 1998)

Barn Cat: A Counting Book (Illustrations only, 1998)

The Tale of John Barleycorn; or, From Barley to Beer (1982)

The Farmer's Alphabet (1981)

The Wild Flavor (Illustrations only, 1973)

Azarian's Major Literary Award

1999 Caldecott Medal
  Snowflake Bentley

she lays paper on the block and rolls a heavy cylinder over it to print the image onto the paper. Finally, she paints in the colors.

Azarian's pictures were published in a cookbook—*The Wild Flavor*, by Marilyn Kluger—in 1973. Sometime later, she heard that the Vermont Council on the Arts was awarding grants to artists to produce artwork that focused on Vermont themes. Azarian remembered the alphabet posters she had made for her little one-room schoolhouse. She began to think about making another set of alphabet posters. For this new set, Azarian had each letter stand for some aspect of rural life in Vermont.

Azarian submitted her idea to the arts council and received

a grant to make the posters. They were a great success! The Vermont Department of Education printed sets of the posters to give to every elementary-school classroom in the state. In 1981, the posters were made into a book called *The Farmer's Alphabet*.

Azarian went on to illustrate many books written by other people. In 2000, she combined her artistic skills with her love of gardening to produce *A Gardener's Alphabet*. Her simple text explores the wonders—and hard work—of gardening.

Today, Azarian lives and works in Plainfield, Vermont, where she still enjoys gardening and creating her unique woodcut prints.

⚬❧

WHERE TO FIND OUT MORE ABOUT MARY AZARIAN

BOOKS

Hart, Lilias MacBean. *The Four Seasons of Mary Azarian*. Boston: David R. Godine, 2000.

McElmeel, Sharron L. *Children's Authors and Illustrators Too Good to Miss: Biographical Sketches and Bibliographies*. Englewood, Colo: Libraries Unlimited, 2004.

Silvey, Anita, ed. *The Essential Guide to Children's Books and Their Creators*. Boston: Houghton Mifflin Company, 2002.

WEB SITES

MARY AZARIAN
http://www.maryazarian.com/
To learn about the artist and order prints and cards from her

NATIONAL CENTER FOR CHILDREN'S ILLUSTRATED LITERATURE
http://www.nccil.org/azarian.html
For a biography and essay about the illustrator

———

AZARIAN READS FOR AN HOUR EVERY MORNING BEFORE BEGINNING HER ARTWORK.

Natalie Babbitt

Born: July 28, 1932

Natalie Babbitt believes in the perfect word. She is fascinated by words, and her book *The Search for Delicious* is devoted to the search for the word *delicious.* The book might sound a little too abstract for a children's book, but it is actually great fun. And it is typical of stories by Natalie Babbitt. She tackles difficult subjects with a sense of amusement and a richness that appeal to children.

It might seem odd that, as a child, such a lover of words never

wanted to be an author. But from a young age, Natalie Babbitt thought only of pictures. She was born Natalie Zane Moore on July 28, 1932, in Dayton, Ohio, during the Great Depression. Her family frequently moved in search of work. Economic security had vanished with the onset of the Great Depression.

Despite the hardships of that era, Natalie enjoyed her childhood. Her parents refused to let the Depression

NATALIE BABBITT DOES NOT BELIEVE PEOPLE CAN BE TAUGHT TO WRITE. SHE SAYS THERE IS ONLY ONE WAY TO BECOME GOOD WITH WORDS AND THAT IS THROUGH LOTS OF READING.

ruin their sense of fun. And her mother, who had hoped to be a writer and artist herself, encouraged Natalie's interest in painting. Natalie fell in love with illustration after seeing John Tenniel's drawings in *Alice in Wonderland*. The whimsical pictures capture the book's sense of unreality, and both qualities appear in her own work.

> *"I am often asked why I do not write books for adults.... Only in a child's book can a writer take advantage of the widest range of symbolism ... and ... have at his disposal the whole vast richness that only fantasy can offer."*

Hoping to become a children's book illustrator, Natalie Moore studied art in college. She first went to the Laurel School in Cleveland, Ohio, and then to Smith College in Northampton, Massachusetts. At that time, she believed she could say what she wanted to say through illustrations. The words could be left to others.

Initially, the words were supplied by her husband, Samuel Fisher Babbitt. Natalie and Samuel collaborated on their first books together. Samuel wrote the words, and Natalie drew the pictures. When Samuel took a job as president of Kirkland College in Upstate New York, however, Natalie was left without an author. She decided to write the books herself.

Her earliest books were *Dick Foote and the Shark* and *Phoebe's Revolt*. In them, she proved that she could write. Even more exciting, she discovered

---

OF HER OWN WRITINGS, BABBITT'S FAVORITE IS *HERBERT ROWBARGE*, ABOUT THE OHIO SHE KNEW GROWING UP. SHE TRIED TO WRITE IT FOR CHILDREN, BUT IT ENDED UP, ACCORDING TO HER, AS A BOOK FOR WOMEN OLDER THAN FORTY.

A Selected Bibliography of Babbitt's Work

Peacock and Other Poems (Illustrations only, 2002)

Elsie Times Eight: A Story and Pictures (2001)

Ouch!: A Tale from Grimm (1998)

Bub, or, The Very Best Thing (1994)

Nellie: A Cat on Her Own (1989)

The Devil's Other Storybook (1987)

Herbert Rowbarge (1982)

The Eyes of the Amaryllis (1977)

Tuck Everlasting (1975)

The Devil's Storybook: Stories and Pictures (1974)

Goody Hall (1971)

Kneeknock Rise (1970)

The Something: Story and Pictures (1970)

The Search for Delicious (1969)

Phoebe's Revolt (1968)

Dick Foote and the Shark (1967)

The Forty-Ninth Magician (Illustrations only, 1966)

Babbitt's Major Literary Award

1971 Newbery Honor Book
  Kneeknock Rise

she could write children's verses that were exceptionally memorable and that sparked the imagination. These were picture books, with texts that enhanced the illustrations. Babbitt had discovered something surprising: she found that she could express ideas in words that she could not express in pictures. She had become a writer. The novels she later wrote for children had pictures that enhanced the story instead of the other way round.

As a writer, she could tackle tricky problems. In *Tuck Everlasting,* she examines the dark side of eternal life. In *The Devil's Storybook: Stories and Pictures,* Babbitt writes hilariously about a devil whose plans to corrupt local townspeople are constantly foiled by the people's goodness. Babbitt has described her own writing as "wordy," but her words weave fabulous stories. Her stories allow children to think while they are being entertained and laugh even when they are reading about dreadful situations.

> *"In the last forty years, people have decided that children can't understand any words that have more than four or five letters. That's just plain crazy. . . . Should we wait until high school to teach words of more than one syllable? No, no, no."*

WHERE TO FIND OUT MORE ABOUT NATALIE BABBITT

BOOKS

Levy, Michael M. *Natalie Babbitt.* New York: Twayne Publishers, 1991.

Pendergast, Sara, and Tom Pendergast, eds. *St. James Guide to Children's Writers.* 5th ed. Detroit: St. James Press, 1999.

Silvey, Anita, ed. *The Essential Guide to Children's Books and Their Creators.* Boston: Houghton Mifflin Company, 2002.

WEB SITES

THE BULLETIN OF THE CENTER FOR CHILDREN'S BOOKS
http://alexia.lis.uiuc.edu/puboff/bccb/0699true.html.
To read biographical information and a discussion of Babbitt's writing

KIDSREADS.COM
http://www.kidsreads.com/authors/au-babbitt-natalie.asp
To read an autobiographical sketch

NATALIE BABBITT WANTED THE SETTING OF *THE EYES OF THE AMARYLLIS,* IN CAPE COD, MASSACHUSETTS, TO BE ACCURATE. SHE WENT SO FAR AS TO LOOK AT OLD TIDAL CHARTS.

Molly Garrett Bang

Born: December 29, 1943

Molly Garrett Bang's work helps prove the saying that myths are universal. A myth deals with the most basic struggles of human life. These include the struggle against nature, the struggle for religious understanding, and the struggle to find meaning in life. Sometimes Bang's characters might seem unfamiliar. And her settings include places as remote as India, Japan, and China. But Bang's vivid illustrations of world myths make the situations familiar. Because of her art, readers can travel to distant lands and discover that their own lives are much like those of Bang's characters.

Bang was exposed to foreign lands and cultures from an early age. She was born on December 29, 1943, in Princeton, New Jersey. Her mother was a translator and her father was a research physician. Her mother's work encouraged Molly Bang's interest in languages.

NOT ALL OF BANG'S BOOKS ARE ADAPTATIONS OF FOLKTALES. IN 1983, SHE PUBLISHED A COUNTING BOOK FOR CHILDREN CALLED *TEN, NINE, EIGHT,* WHICH COUNTS DOWN THE TIME BEFORE A YOUNG GIRL FALLS ASLEEP.

As an adult, Bang has worked with her mother on creating books for children.

Bang attended Wellesley College in Wellesley, Massachusetts. She majored in French but was also interested in the arts. The style of Japanese painters and wood-block carvers particularly caught her imagination. Some Japanese prints are delicate and subtle, while others depict dramatic scenes through bursts of color and action. After graduating from Wellesley, Bang moved to Japan, where she taught English and studied Japanese.

When Bang returned to the United States, she continued to study Asia at the University of Arizona and Harvard University. Her Japanese studies led to a

A Selected Bibliography of Bang's Work

Little Rat Plays the Violin (2006)
My Light (2004)
Little Rat Sets Sail (2002)
Tiger's Fall (2001)
Nobody Particular: One Woman's Fight to Save the Bays (2000)
When Sophie Gets Angry—Really, Really Angry . . . (1999)
Common Ground: The Water, Earth, and Air We Share (1997)
Goose (1996)
One Fall Day (1994)
Yellow Ball (1991)
Delphine (1988)
The Paper Crane (1985)
Dawn (1983)
Ten, Nine, Eight (1983)
The Grey Lady and the Strawberry Snatcher (1980)
Wiley and the Hairy Man: Adapted from an American Folktale (1976)
The Goblins Giggle and Other Stories (Selected and illustrated, 1973)

Bang's Major Literary Awards

2002 Boston Globe-Horn Book Picture Book Honor Book
 Little Rat Sets Sail

2000 Caldecott Honor Book
 When Sophie Gets Angry—Really, Really Angry . . .

1986 Boston Globe-Horn Book Picture Book Award
 The Paper Crane

1984 Boston Globe-Horn Book Picture Book Honor Book
 Dawn

1984 Caldecott Honor Book
 Ten, Nine, Eight

1981 Caldecott Honor Book

1980 Boston Globe-Horn Book Picture Book Honor Book
 The Grey Lady and the Strawberry Snatcher

stint as a translator for the New York City office of a Japanese newspaper. In 1974, she married Richard H. Campbell, and the two later had a daughter, Monika.

During her time in Japan, Bang studied the folklore of Japan. She began creating drawings that the stories suggested. In Japanese style, she painted the demons, warriors, and court ladies of Japanese tales. When she showed them to a publisher, she was told that they were too scary for children. She went to another publisher who published them in a book called *The Goblins Giggle and Other Stories.* They might have scared the publisher, but children love them.

> *"I'm convinced by all I've seen that every one of us is indeed an artist, if we only have the tools."*

Many of Bang's early books have Asian themes. She has retold the legends of China and Japan using her own stunning illustrations. Occasionally, she has transferred an Asian folktale into an American setting. A Japanese crane, for example, is replaced by a Canada goose in her book *Goose.*

It seems that wherever Bang has traveled, books have resulted. She spent a year in India working for a United Nations relief organization and a year in the African country of Mali as a civil servant. She later illustrated folktales from India and Africa. But her curiosity about folklore has not been limited to foreign cultures. In her research for *Wiley*

BANG GETS INVOLVED IN THE PLACES SHE LIVES. IN HER CURRENT HOME OF WOODS HOLE, MASSACHUSETTS, SHE HAS BEEN THE EDITOR OF THE *WOODS HOLE PASSAGE* AND A TRUSTEE OF THE WOODS HOLE COMMUNITY ASSOCIATION.

and the Hairy Man, she traveled through the American South on a motorcycle, getting a sense of both the landscape and the culture. Through her own artistic vision, Molly Bang has brought the tales of the countries she has visited a little closer to her readers.

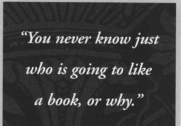

"You never know just who is going to like a book, or why."

❧

WHERE TO FIND OUT MORE ABOUT MOLLY GARRETT BANG

BOOKS

Kovacs, Deborah, and James Preller. *Meet the Authors and Illustrators: 60 Creators of Favorite Children's Books Talk about Their Work.* Vol. 2. New York: Scholastic, 1993.

McElmeel, Sharron L. *100 Most Popular Picture Book Authors and Illustrators: Biographical Sketches and Bibliographies.* Englewood, Colo.: Libraries Unlimited, 2000.

WEB SITES

BETWEEN THE LINES
http://www.harcourtbooks.com/authorinterviews/bookinterview_Bang-Campbell.asp
To read an interview with Molly Bang and her daughter, writer Monika Bang-Campbell

MOLLY BANG HOME PAGE
http://www.mollybang.com/
For a selection of illustrations and descriptions of books by Bang

WHILE IN INDIA, BANG ILLUSTRATED HEALTH MANUALS THAT WERE GIVEN OUT IN VILLAGES WHERE MANY PEOPLE COULD NOT READ. HER PICTURES BECAME A TOOL FOR IMPROVING THE HEALTH OF LOCAL RESIDENTS.

Lynne Reid Banks

Born: July 31, 1929

As a young girl, Lynne Reid Banks loved to write. It was something that came very easily to her. But her dream was to be an actress. After acting for five years, Banks went on to become a successful writer of both adult and children's books. Her best-known children's books include *The Indian in the Cupboard* and *The Secret of the Indian.*

Banks was born on July 31, 1929, in London, England. When she was about ten years old, World War II (1939–1945) began. Nazi forces threatened to invade Britain. Lynne, together with her mother and a boy cousin, were evacuated to the Canadian prairies, where they lived for nearly five years.

When she returned to Britain at age fifteen, Lynne was shocked at what she saw. Many parts of London were flattened, as

---

BANKS HAS SERVED AS A VOLUNTEER TEACHER OF ENGLISH AS A SECOND LANGUAGE IN TANZANIA, ZIMBABWE, INDIA, AND NEPAL.

were many other ports and major cities. She felt bad when she heard the stories from people who stayed in England. She felt like a deserter, even though she couldn't help having left.

At seventeen, Banks began attending the Royal Academy of Dramatic Art. Then she worked as an actress, but it was difficult for her to find regular work. Banks went into journalism and eventually got a job as a TV news reporter. She was one of the first two woman TV news reporters in Britain.

> *"The trick of writing fiction is much akin to the trick of good acting. You have to get into other minds, speak through other mouths, move with other bodies, feel with other hearts. Of course it helps if you can write well."*

Banks also wrote plays and novels for adults. Her first novel for adults was *The L-Shaped Room,* which was later filmed. It was published in the United States in 1961.

In 1962, Banks moved to Israel, where she married a sculptor and had three sons—Adiel, Gillon, and Omri. While living on a collective farm called a kibbutz in Israel, she did farm work and then became a teacher of English to Hebrew-speaking children. Her training as an actress helped her in her job. "Every lesson was a performance," Banks says. "How else could I make them understand me? And it worked. I was more successful at teaching than I ever was on the stage."

BANKS'S BOOK *THE INDIAN IN THE CUPBOARD* WAS ADAPTED INTO A MOTION PICTURE THAT WAS RELEASED IN **1995.**

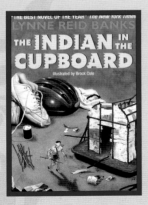

A Selected Bibliography of Banks's Work

Harry the Poisonous Centipede Goes to Sea (2006)

Tiger, Tiger (2005)

The Dungeon (2002)

Harry the Poisonous Centipede's Big Adventure: Another Story to Make You Squirm (2001)

Alice by Accident (2000)

Key to the Indian (1998)

Maura's Angel (1998)

Moses in Egypt: A Novel Inspired by the Book of Exodus and the Prince of Egypt (1998)

Angela and Diabola (1997)

Harry the Poisonous Centipede: A Story to Make You Squirm (1997)

Broken Bridge (1994)

Magic Hare (1993)

The Mystery of the Cupboard (1993)

The Secret of the Indian (1989)

The Fairy Rebel (1988)

The Return of the Indian (1986)

The Indian in the Cupboard (1980)

Letters to My Israeli Sons (1979)

I, Houdini: The Autobiography of a Self-Educated Hamster (1978)

Path to the Silent Country: A Sequel to Dark Quartet (1978)

Dark Quartet: The Story of the Brontës (1976)

The Farthest-Away Mountain (1976)

The Adventures of King Midas (1976)

One More River (1971)

Banks and her family returned to Britain in 1971. That year, her first book for young adults, *One More River,* was published. Her memories of living in Canada as a teenager and her experiences in Israel contributed to this book. Since that time, she has written more than thirty books for adults and children.

"I never set out to write a 'message book,' because the function of the novelist is to tell stories, to involve the reader in the lives of made-up characters. But inevitably, my personal philosophy . . . informs everything I do, and occasionally my own opinions and feelings creep in."

Banks has found that she enjoys writing for young people more than adults. "Writing for young people is a much pleasanter, and easier, thing than writing for adults," Banks says. "I especially enjoy writing wish-fulfillment tales for younger children."

Lynne Reid Banks lives in England. She continues to write for adults and young readers.

> *"The thought that my books might go on being read after I'm gone is more exciting to me than going to heaven. It's the only kind of immortality I recognize."*

WHERE TO FIND OUT MORE ABOUT LYNNE REID BANKS

BOOKS

Berger, Laura Stanley, ed. *Twentieth-Century Young Adult Writers.* Detroit: St. James, 1994.

Silvey, Anita, ed. The Essential Guide to *Children's Books and Their Creators.* Boston: Houghton Mifflin, 2002.

WEB SITES

HARPER CHILDRENS
http://www.harperchildrens.com/teacher/catalog/author_xml.asp?authorID=11768
For a short biography and links to Banks's works

LYNNE REID BANKS HOME PAGE
http://www.lynnereidbanks.com/
To find information about Banks's books, to read an interview
with the author, and to hear audio samples of selected works

WHEN SHE WAS AN ACTRESS, BANKS BEGAN WRITING PLAYS. SHE WROTE
HER FIRST PLAY WHEN SHE WAS TWENTY-FOUR. SEVERAL OF HER
WORKS WERE PRODUCED IN THEATERS OR ON TELEVISION.

Joan Bauer

Born: July 12, 1951

Like many of her characters, Joan Bauer faced her share of problems growing up. Now she puts those problems to good use in her young-adult novels. "The theme that I try to carry into all of my writing," she says, "is this: adversity, if we let it, will make us stronger."

Joan was born in Oak Park, Illinois, in 1951. She grew up in nearby River Forest and was the oldest of three girls. As an overweight child, she recalls that she "desperately wanted to be popular." Joan's father was an alcoholic, and her parents divorced when she was eight. Her mother, an English teacher, raised Joan and her sisters.

Joan was especially close to her grandmother, Nana, who lived with the family. She told the girls wonderful stories that made them laugh, even during the tough times. From Nana, Joan learned lifelong lessons about storytelling and the importance of humor.

IN SCHOOL, JOAN DID POORLY IN GYM, BUT SHE WAS GOOD AT WRITING AND LOVED LATIN AND DRAMA.

As a child, Joan wrote stories and poems. She played the flute and taught herself to play the guitar. She was an avid reader and loved visiting the public library. When Joan was a teenager, her beloved Nana developed Alzheimer's disease. Then in 1971, her father committed suicide. Her struggle with his life and death would ultimately have an impact on her writing. "Every book I have written so far has dealt with complex father issues," she says.

In her early twenties, she began selling advertising for companies such as the *Chicago Tribune*, WLS radio, and *Parade* magazine. She married Evan Bauer, a computer engineer, in 1981. They settled in south-western Connecticut, and their

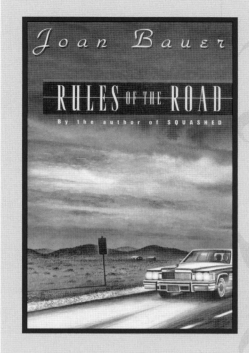

A Selected Bibliography of Bauer's Work

Best Foot Forward (2005)
Stand Tall (2002)
Hope Was Here (2000)
Backwater (1999)
Rules of the Road (1998)
Sticks (1996)
Thwonk (1995)
Squashed (1992)

Bauer's Major Literary Award

2001 Newbery Honor Book
  Hope Was Here

"Over the years, I have come to understand how deeply I need to laugh. It's like oxygen to me. My best times as a writer are when I'm working on a book and laughing while I'm writing. Then I know I've got something."

daughter, Jean, was born in 1982. When Jean was a baby, Bauer wrote articles that appeared in *American Baby* magazine. This was her first published work.

After selling advertising for ten years, Bauer was frustrated. She had no opportunity for creativity, and the pressure of the job was affecting her health. "It was then that I finally began to listen to my heart, quit my job, and started writing," she recalls. Her first book, *Squashed*, came out in 1992, and more followed. Bauer's daughter was a great help to this new career. Jean kept her mom in touch with the current youth culture, read her manuscripts, and gave her tips.

Bauer's novels address serious issues, but they maintain a lighthearted touch. Most of her leading characters have a special talent. That talent may be raising pumpkins, shooting pool, or selling shoes. Yet their abilities lead them in surprising directions. Along the way, Bauer's characters encounter dark truths, suffer disappointments, learn their strengths, and emerge much wiser than they start out.

"Stories have always helped me to understand life. When I'm writing a story, I'm really exploring how I feel about the world. I'm working things out in fiction and metaphor—things that I believe to be true."

JOAN'S FAVORITE BOOK AS A CHILD WAS *TO KILL A MOCKINGBIRD* BY HARPER LEE. SHE LIKED IT SO MUCH BECAUSE SHE FELT IT PRESENTED A GOOD FATHER FIGURE.

A dash of humor always makes the characters' journeys easier. In *Rules of the Road*, for example, a teenage girl takes a long road trip with her boss. After dealing with heartbreak and treachery, she muses, "Somebody should stick up some signs on the highway of life. 'CAUTION: JERKS CROSSING.'"

Bauer lives in Brooklyn, New York, with her husband. She enjoys cooking, reading, exploring New York City, and listening to jazz and classical music.

WHERE TO FIND OUT MORE ABOUT JOAN BAUER

BOOKS

Koehler-Pentacoff, Elizabeth. *The ABC's of Writing for Children*. Sanger, Calif.: Quill Driver Books, 2003.

Rockman, Connie C., ed. *Eighth Book of Junior Authors & Illustrators*. New York: H. W. Wilson, 2000.

Silvey, Anita, ed. *The Essential Guide to Children's Books and Their Creators*. Boston: Houghton Mifflin Company, 2002.

WEB SITES

CHILDREN'S BOOK PAGE
http://www.bookpage.com/0507bp/children/best_foot_forward.html
To read an interview and review of *Best Foot Forward*

JOAN BAUER
http://www.joanbauer.com/jbbooks.html
To read about her books

JOAN LEARNED TO PLAY POOL WHEN SHE WAS A TEENAGER. SHE USED THAT EXPERIENCE IN HER NOVEL *STICKS*, WHICH TELLS THE STORY OF A BOY WHO'S PREPARING FOR A BIG POOL TOURNAMENT.

L. Frank Baum

Born: May 15, 1856
Died: May 6, 1919

Before he began writing stories, L. Frank Baum ran a general store in Aberdeen, South Dakota. The store was always crowded, but not with customers. Instead, it was children who flocked to the store to hear the shopkeeper tell his fantastic tales. Business was so slow that Baum had plenty of time to spend telling the children stories. In fact, it wasn't long before Baum left the storekeeping business and began writing down some of his stories for children. One of them, called "The Emerald City," became one of the best-selling stories of all time. We know it as *The Wonderful Wizard of Oz.*

Lyman Frank Baum was born on May 15, 1856, in Chittenango, New York. Frank was the seventh child born to Benjamin and Cynthia Stanton Baum. As a boy, he suffered from a painful heart disease called angina pectoris. Stuck at home because of his illness, Frank came to love reading fairy tales and stories by English novelist Charles Dickens. At

L. FRANK BAUM'S FIRST PUBLISHED BOOK, CALLED *THE BOOK OF HAMBURGS*, WAS ABOUT A SMALL, COLORFUL BREED OF CHICKEN.

fifteen, he started his own newspaper, using a small printing press his father had bought him. He even sold advertising space in the paper to local merchants.

Frank Baum also became interested in acting and the theater. As a teenager, he memorized entire scenes from plays by William Shakespeare. As an adult, he traveled to New York and worked briefly as an actor. Later, Baum managed several small theaters in Upstate New York. In 1880, he began writing plays.

Also around that time, he met Maud Gage, a student at Cornell University in Ithaca, New York. The two fell in love and were married on November 9, 1882.

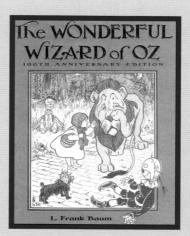

A Selected Bibliography of Baum's Work
Glinda of Oz (1920)
The Tin Woodman of Oz (1918)
The Lost Princess of Oz (1917)
The Scarecrow of Oz (1915)
The Patchwork Girl of Oz (1913)
The Emerald City of Oz (1910)
The Road to Oz (1909)
Dorothy and the Wizard of Oz (1908)
Ozma of Oz (1907)
The Life and Adventures of Santa Claus (1902)
The Wonderful Wizard of Oz (1900)
Father Goose: His Book (1899)
Mother Goose in Prose (1897)

The Baums moved to what is now South Dakota in 1888. (At the time, South Dakota was part of the Dakota Territory. It became a state in 1889.) After his general store failed, Baum worked as a reporter for a newspaper in Aberdeen.

In 1893, the Baums moved to Chicago, where he wrote for the *Evening Post* and worked as a traveling salesman. In 1897, Frank Baum published his first children's book. Called *Mother Goose in Prose,* it was based on the stories Baum enjoyed telling local children. He followed that book with *Father Goose: His Book* in 1899, which became the best-selling children's book of that year.

> *"While Dorothy was looking earnestly into the queer, painted face of the Scarecrow, she was surprised to see one of the eyes slowly wink at her. She thought she must have been mistaken at first, for none of the scarecrows in Kansas ever wink; but presently the figure nodded its head to her in a friendly way."*
>
> —*from* **The Wonderful Wizard of Oz**

In 1900, Baum sent his publisher a new story titled "The Emerald City." The publisher liked the story but suggested a new title. So the story was published as *The Wonderful Wizard of Oz.* It told the story of a farm girl named Dorothy and her dog, Toto, who are transported to a strange, magical land by a whirling tornado.

THREE YEARS BEFORE *THE WONDERFUL WIZARD OF OZ* WAS PUBLISHED, A FARM GIRL NAMED DOROTHY APPEARED IN BAUM'S BOOK *MOTHER GOOSE IN PROSE.*

The Wonderful Wizard of Oz was a huge hit. Readers loved it so much that they demanded more and more stories about Dorothy, Toto, and the land of Oz. Eventually, Baum wrote more than a dozen books, a play, and even several early movies about Oz. Even after he died, other writers continued to produce books about Oz.

The success of the book changed Baum's life. For the first time, he was able to devote himself to writing full-time. He moved to Hollywood, where he lived in a house he called Ozcot. His poor health continued to be a problem, however. He died on May 6, 1919, after an operation on his gallbladder. But his fanciful stories of Dorothy and Oz live on in books, in movies, and on television.

☙

WHERE TO FIND OUT MORE ABOUT L. FRANK BAUM

BOOKS

Greene, Carol. *L. Frank Baum: Author of the Wonderful Wizard of Oz*.
Chicago: Childrens Press, 1995.

Rahn, Suzanne. *The Wizard of Oz: Shaping an Imaginary World*.
New York: Twayne Publishers, 1998.

Wheeler, Jill C. *L. Frank Baum*. Edina, Minn.: Abdo & Daughters, 1997.

WEB SITE

THE MAN BEHIND THE CURTAIN: L. FRANK BAUM AND THE WIZARD OF OZ
http://www.literarytraveler.com/spring/west/baum.htm
To read a detailed biography of L. Frank Baum

———

BAUM WROTE OTHER BOOKS UNDER PSEUDONYMS, OR FALSE NAMES. HIS
PSEUDONYMS INCLUDED EDITH VAN DYNE AND LAURA BANCROFT.

John Bellairs

Born: January 17, 1938
Died: March 8, 1991

John Bellairs once said, "Writing seems to be [for me] a way of memorializing and transforming my own past." Certainly that is true of the settings of Bellairs's spooky mysteries. Bellairs created three series of books. Each takes place in a different fictional town. And each town bears a strong resemblance to a place where Bellairs had lived.

The first series started in 1973 with *The House with a Clock in Its Walls,* his first children's book. It continued with *The Figure in the Shadows* and *The Letter, the Witch, and the Ring.* These books focus on Lewis Barnavelt, a young boy whose parents have been killed in an auto accident. He goes to live with his Uncle Jonathan, who lives in an old house full of mysterious passages and surprises. There he meets Uncle Jonathan's neighbor, Mrs. Zimmermann, who turns out to be a

WHEN JOHN BELLAIRS DIED, HE LEFT BEHIND TWO PARTLY COMPLETED BOOKS AND TWO OUTLINES. THESE WERE COMPLETED BY A FAN OF BELLAIRS'S NAMED BRAD STRICKLAND, WHO HAS GONE ON TO WRITE ORIGINAL NOVELS USING BELLAIRS'S CHARACTERS.

wizard—just like Uncle Jonathan. They are forced to battle against evils from out of the past in the little town of New Zebedee.

New Zebedee, with its big, strange old houses and its sense of history, is modeled on Marshall, Michigan, where John Bellairs was born on January 17, 1938. *The House with a Clock in Its Walls* is based on Cronin House in Marshall. John's father owned a saloon, and business wasn't always good. John Bellairs remembered his parents' worries. In Bellairs's books, children often get into trouble while trying to make their families more financially secure.

In 1959, Bellairs graduated from the University of Notre Dame in Indiana. He then studied for his master's degree at the University of Chicago. He became an English teacher at the College of St. Teresa in Winona, Minnesota. Years later, Winona would be the model for Hoosac, Minnesota, in the series of books featuring Anthony Monday and his brave librarian friend, Myra Eells. This series included *The Treasure of Alpheus Winterborn* and *The Dark Secret of Weatherend*.

Bellairs worked as a teacher for seven years until 1966. Then he quit to write full-time, only to discover that he couldn't yet make

> *"I love ghost stories, coffins, bones, spells, Latin, cathedrals, darkness, castles, England, cobalt blue, Christmas, Italian food, the moon, secret passages, and wizards like Gandalf. I'm also a Red Sox fan."*

IN 1993, A NEW COMPUTER VIRUS WAS NAMED FOR THE FUSE BOX DWARF, A CHARACTER IN JOHN BELLAIRS'S *THE HOUSE WITH A CLOCK IN ITS WALLS*. INCLUDED IN THE VIRUS'S PROGRAMMING WAS THE DWARF'S CRY IN THE BOOK, "DREEB! DREEB! I AM THE FUSE BOX DWARF."

A Selected Bibliography of Bellairs's Work

The Doom of the Haunted Opera (1995)

The Drum, the Doll, and the Zombie (1994)

The Vengeance of the Witch-Finder (1993)

The Mansion in the Mist (1992)

The Secret of the Underground Room (1990)

Chessmen of Doom (1989)

The Trolley to Yesterday (1989)

The Lamp from the Warlock's Tomb (1988)

The Revenge of the Wizard's Ghost (1985)

The Dark Secret of Weatherend (1984)

The Spell of the Sorcerer's Skull (1984)

The Curse of the Blue Figurine (1983)

The Mummy, the Will, and the Crypt (1983)

The Treasure of Alpheus Winterborn (1978)

The Letter, the Witch, and the Ring (1976)

The Figure in the Shadows (1975)

The House with a Clock in Its Walls (1973)

The Face in the Frost (1969)

The Pedant and the Shuffly (1968)

his living that way. His most successful book for adults was *The Face in the Frost.* It helped Bellairs discover the kind of story he would tell for the rest of his life—mysterious, spooky, and funny, with real scares and real laughs.

By this time, Bellairs was married, and he moved with his wife, Priscilla, to New England. They eventually settled in North Andover, Massachusetts. Bellairs turned North Andover into the setting for the Blue Figurine books, starring Johnny Dixon. He started teaching again while working on something new—a children's book. This time, success came. His mysteries became extremely popular, and several were turned into television movies. At last, Bellairs was able to stop teaching and write full-time.

Bellairs and his wife divorced in the 1980s. Bellairs died of a heart attack in 1991.

> *"All . . . of my children's books are autobiographical. They're a combination of the everyday and the fantastic. The common ordinary stuff—the bullies, the scaredy-cat kid Lewis, the grown-ups, the everyday incidents—all come from my own experience."*

WHERE TO FIND OUT MORE ABOUT JOHN BELLAIRS

BOOKS

Clute, John, and John Grant, eds. *The Encyclopedia of Fantasy.* New York: St. Martin's Press, 1997.

McElmeel, Sharron L. *100 Most Popular Children's Authors: Biographical Sketches and Bibliographies.* Englewood, Colo.: Libraries Unlimited, 1999.

Silvey, Anita, ed. *The Essential Guide to Children's Books and Their Creators.* Boston: Houghton Mifflin Company, 2002.

WEB SITE

BELLAIRSIA
http://www.bellairsia.com
For biographical information and photographs of John Bellairs, a booklist, and a timeline

WHEN BELLAIRS WAS IN COLLEGE, HE REPRESENTED THE UNIVERSITY OF NOTRE DAME ON *COLLEGE BOWL*, A TV QUIZ SHOW FEATURING COLLEGE TEAMS. HIS BEST ACHIEVEMENT WAS RECOGNIZING THE BEGINNING OF GEOFFREY CHAUCER'S CLASSIC POEM *THE CANTERBURY TALES* AFTER HEARING ONLY TWO WORDS OF IT.

Ludwig Bemelmans

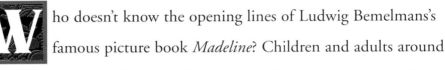

Born: April 27, 1898
Died: October 1, 1962

Who doesn't know the opening lines of Ludwig Bemelmans's famous picture book *Madeline*? Children and adults around the world can recite: "In an old house in Paris that was covered with vines, lived twelve little girls in two straight lines." Using rhyming words and whimsical illustrations, Bemelmans made Madeline, Mademoiselle Clavel, and the city of Paris come to vivid life for millions of fans.

Ludwig Bemelmans didn't start out to be a famous writer and artist. In fact, for a while his family wondered if he would ever be anything but a troublemaker! Ludwig Bemelmans was born on April 27, 1898, in a hotel room in Meran, Tyrol, Austria. (This area is now a part of Italy.) His parents were divorced when he was eight, and Ludwig was sent to live with his mother's mother in Germany.

LUDWIG BEMELMANS OFTEN SAID THAT HE WROTE BOOKS BECAUSE HE HAD INSOMNIA. IF HE COULD SLEEP WELL, HE WOULD NEVER WRITE AGAIN!

Ludwig was a rebellious child and teenager. He didn't do well at school, so his family sent him to work for an uncle who owned several hotels. Ludwig didn't do well at hotels, either. When he finally got into a bad fight with another waiter, his family gave him a choice: go to reform school, or go to America.

Ludwig chose America. He arrived in New York in 1914, when he was just sixteen years old. He found—and was fired from—a series of hotel jobs.

> *"My first job in New York, at the Hotel Astor, did not last long. I filled water bottles and carried out trays with dishes, until I broke too many."*

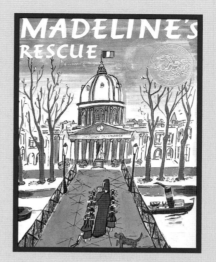

A Selected Bibliography of Bemelmans's Work

Madeline in America and Other Holiday Tales (1999)
Mad about Madeline: The Complete Tales (1993)
Rosebud (1993)
Madeline's Christmas (1985)
Marina (1962)
Madeline in London (1961)
Madeline and the Gypsies (1959)
Madeline and the Bad Hat (1956)
Parsley (1955)
Madeline's Rescue (1953)
Fifi (1940)
Madeline (1939)
Quito Express (1938)
Noodle (1937)
The Golden Basket (1936)
Hansi (1934)

Bemelmans's Major Literary Awards

1954 Caldecott Medal
Madeline's Rescue

1940 Caldecott Honor Book
Madeline

1937 Newbery Honor Book
The Golden Basket

> *"I have repeatedly said two things that no one takes seriously, and they are that first of all I am not a writer but a painter, and secondly that I have no imagination. It is very curious that, with my lack of these important essentials, the character of Madeline came to be."*

In 1917, he enlisted in the U.S. Army. The following year he became a U.S. citizen.

After his army service ended, Bemelmans returned to hotel and restaurant work. He also started drawing and taking art lessons. When he opened his own restaurant in 1925, he covered the walls with huge murals.

People noticed these murals. They also noticed the bright and funny pictures he painted all over the walls of his apartment. It wasn't long before Bemelmans started getting work as a free-lance illustrator. In 1934, he published his first book for children. *Hansi* was written from his own childhood memories and illustrated with watercolor drawings.

For years, Bemelmans had remembered the stories his mother had told him about her life as a little girl in a convent school. He was inspired by these stories—and by his wife, Madeline, and his daughter, Barbara— to create the first Madeline book. The idea for Madeline's burst appendix came when Bemelmans went to the hospital after a bicycle accident. In the hospital room across the hall was a little girl who proudly showed him the scar from her appendix operation!

LUDWIG BEMELMANS IS MOST FAMOUS FOR HIS MADELINE SERIES OF PICTURE BOOKS. BUT HE ALSO WROTE BOOKS AND MAGAZINE ARTICLES ON TRAVEL, COOKING, AND HIS LIFE'S ADVENTURES. HIS ARTWORK WAS SHOWN IN NEW YORK GALLERIES, AND HE DREW MANY MAGAZINE COVERS.

Madeline became immediately popular when it was published in 1939. It was named a Caldecott Honor Book in 1940 and has been made into several movies. The second book in the series, *Madeline's Rescue,* won the Caldecott Medal in 1954. In all, Bemelmans wrote six books about his spirited Parisian schoolgirl. Today, you can find Madeline dolls, Madeline lunch boxes, Madeline backpacks—and, of course, the unforgettable Madeline books!

Ludwig Bemelmans was working on a seventh Madeline book when he died on October 1, 1962. He was sixty-four years old.

ॐ

WHERE TO FIND OUT MORE ABOUT LUDWIG BEMELMANS

BOOKS

Eastman, Jacqueline Fisher. *Ludwig Bemelmans.* New York: Twayne, 1996.

Marciano, John Bemelmans. *Bemelmans: The Life and Art of Madeline's Creator.* New York: Viking, 1999.

WEB SITES

KIDSREADS.COM
http://www.kidsreads.com/series/series-madeline-author.asp
For a biography and selected booklist for Ludwig Bemelmans

MADELINE
http://www.madeline.com/
To read about the books and characters in the Madeline series

―――

WHEN TWO YOUNG NEIGHBORS ASKED BEMELMANS FOR A SECOND MADELINE BOOK, HE OFFERED THEM FIFTY CENTS FOR AN IDEA. THEY SUGGESTED THAT MADELINE GET A DOG. BEMELMANS TOOK THE IDEA AND WROTE *MADELINE'S RESCUE.*

Stan Berenstain
Jan Berenstain

Born: September 29, 1923 (Stan)   Died: November 26, 2005 (Stan)
Born: July 26, 1923 (Jan)

It should be no surprise that Stan and Jan Berenstain's most famous books are about a family. They were happily married for fifty-nine years. Their Berenstain Bears books reflect the same struggles and comedies they themselves experienced while raising their two children, Leo and Michael. They have described themselves as a Mom and Pop shop of children's books.

The Berenstains' lives were remarkably similar from the beginning. Both were born in Philadelphia, Pennsylvania, in 1923. Jan was born Janice Grant on July 26, and Stan was born on September 29. They grew up during the Great Depression, when millions of Americans were out of work and the economy was in ruins. Jan's family lost its building business.

IN 1987, THE BERENSTAINS' FAMILY BUSINESS ADDED A NEW MEMBER. MICHAEL BERENSTAIN ILLUSTRATED *THE DAY OF THE DINOSAUR*, ONE OF THE BERENSTAIN BEARS BOOKS WRITTEN BY HIS PARENTS.

Her father worked as a carpenter and spent much time at home sketching and designing his projects. Jan remembers those days as not so depressing, however. She loved having her father around and dabbling with his drawing tools.

As a child, Stan liked to paint. He especially liked to paint on the walls of his house. He remembers that his first masterpiece was a picture of boxers that he painted on the dining-room wall. His parents were a little upset with Stan's independent decorations. After that, he painted on the cardboard that came with his father's shirts from the laundry.

> *"[We are an] old-fashioned Mom and Pop operation in which both partners do whatever needs to be done—writing, illustrating, cooking, bottle-washing. We find our work (and our bears) tremendously stimulating and enjoyable."*
> —**Stan Berenstain**

The couple met while studying at the Philadelphia College of Art. As soon as Stan finished his degree in 1942, he was drafted into the U.S. Army. While still in the army, Stan started to sketch cartoon drawings. He also submitted cartoons to the *Saturday Review of Literature.* Once the magazine began accepting them, he realized he could make money sketching.

During World War II (1939–1945), Jan volunteered to work as an aircraft riveter and draftsman, while continuing to work on her sketches.

———

THE BERENSTAIN BEARS HAVE PROVEN TOO LIVELY TO STAY IN A BOOK. THEIR ADVENTURES ARE NOW BROADCAST ON TELEVISION, AND MANY BERENSTAIN BEARS SPECIALS HAVE BEEN BROADCAST FOR CHRISTMAS AND OTHER HOLIDAYS.

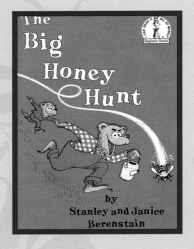

A Selected Bibliography of the Berenstains' Work

The Berenstain Bears and Too Much Car Trip (2006)

The Berenstain Bears and the Baby Chipmunk (2005)

The Berenstain Bears by the Sea (2003)

Down a Sunny Dirt Road (2002)

The Berenstain Bears' Report Card Trouble (2002)

Ride Like the Wind (2002)

The Berensatin Bears and the Excuse Note (2001)

The Berenstain Bears and Baby Makes Five (2000)

The Berenstain Bears and the Big Question (1999)

The Berenstain Bear Scouts and the Missing Merit Badges (1998)

The Berenstain Bears and Queenie's Crazy Crush (1997)

The Berenstain Bear Scouts and the Sci-Fi Pizza (1996)

The Berenstain Bears in the Freaky Funhouse (1995)

The Berenstain Bears' New Neighbors (1994)

The Berenstain Bears and the Bully (1993)

The Berenstain Bears and the Broken Piggy Bank (1992)

The Berenstain Bears Visit the Dentist (1991)

The Berenstain Bears and the Prize Pumpkin (1990)

The Berenstain Bears Forget Their Manners (1985)

The Berenstain Bears Learn about Strangers (1985)

The Berenstain Bears Meet Santa Bear (1984)

The Berenstain Bears and the Truth (1983)

The Berenstain Bears Go to the Doctor (1981)

The Berenstain Bears' New Baby (1974)

The Big Honey Hunt (1962)

After Stan was discharged from the army, he married Jan and the two decided to pool their talents. They designed magazine and book covers as well as cartoons, often about family life. One of their first projects, *It's All in the Family,* was published in *McCall's* and then in *Good Housekeeping.* After their sons were born, they turned to children's books.

As parents, the Berenstains had become interested in the way children learn. They combined their pictures with simple, funny

> *"I see us in the Peter Rabbit mold, popular, gentle, straightforward, and noncontroversial, yet we don't sugar-coat life. We deal with reality."*
> —Stan Berenstain

stories written in rhyme about a family of bears. The books explore real-life situations such as learning to ride a bicycle, going to school, and getting a new baby brother or sister. The Berenstain Bears also have adventures, accidents, and get into trouble.

In a series of "first-time" books, the Berenstains showed the Berenstain Bears encountering new situations for the first time. They go to the dentist, get into a fight, go to camp—all for the first time. The Berenstains, through their bears, have created a guide to childhood, and children have had a good time watching the little bears tumble through all their mishaps.

❧

WHERE TO FIND OUT MORE ABOUT STAN AND JAN BERENSTAIN

BOOKS

Berg, Julie. *The Berenstains: The Young at Heart.* Edina, Minn.: Abdo and Daughters, 1993.

Silvey, Anita, ed. *Children's Books and Their Creators.* Boston: Houghton Mifflin, 1995.

WEB SITES

KIDSREAD.COM
http://www.kidsreads.com/authors/au-berenstain-jan-stan.asp
For a biographical sketch about Stan and Jan Berenstain

THE OFFICIAL BERENSTAIN BEARS WEB SITE
http://www.berenstainbears.com/
To read information on the characters and books in the Berenstain Bears series

———

THE BERENSTAINS DON'T BELIEVE IN UNLUCKY DAYS! STAN WAS DISCHARGED FROM THE ARMY ON APRIL FOOL'S DAY, AND THE COUPLE WERE MARRIED ON THE THIRTEENTH, A DAY MOST PEOPLE TEND TO AVOID.

Quentin Blake

Born: December 16, 1932

Quentin Blake's illustrations are sometimes serious and thought-provoking, but more often they are comic and even zany. His lively artwork appears in more than 250 books enjoyed by both children and adults.

Quentin Saxby Blake was born in 1932 in Sidcup, Kent, a suburb of London, England. As a child, he was an avid reader, although he had few illustrated books besides comic books. In primary school, he loved drawing pictures on the backs of his school notebooks.

Quentin attended Chiselhurst and Sidcup Grammar School. (In England, most grammar schools are secondary schools.) He often submitted stories and illustrations to the school magazine, the *Chronicle*. While at Chiselhurst, he met cartoonist Alfred Jackson, who taught Quentin how to submit drawings to professional magazines. Quentin followed Jackson's advice, and his art appeared

THE BRITISH POSTAL SERVICE USED BLAKE'S PICTURES FOR CHARLES DICKENS'S *A CHRISTMAS CAROL* ON ITS 1997 CHRISTMAS POSTAGE STAMPS.

in the British magazine *Punch* when he was only sixteen.

Military duty was required in England at that time, so Blake served in the Army Education Corps from 1951 to 1953. During this period, he illustrated a book that helped illiterate soldiers learn how to read.

Blake's parents did not encourage him to study art. They wanted him to pursue a more secure profession, something like banking or teaching. When his military service was up, he enrolled in Cambridge University, where he focused on literature. After receiving a master's degree in English in 1956, Blake did a year of teacher training at the University of London. He never took a teaching job,

A Selected Bibliography of Blake's Work

The Life of Birds (2005)

Michael Rosen's Sad Book (Illustrations only, 2005)

Mrs. Armitage: Queen of the Road (2003)

Wizzil (Illustrations only, 2000)

Mrs. Armitage on Wheels (1998)

Zagazoo (1998)

A Christmas Carol (Illustrations only, 1995)

James and the Giant Peach (Illustrations only, 1995)

Charlie and the Chocolate Factory (Illustrations only, 1995)

Clown (1995)

Matilda (Illustrations only, 1988)

How the Camel Got His Hump (Illustrations only, 1984)

The Story of the Dancing Frog (1984)

Mortimer's Cross (Illustrations only, 1983)

The BFG (Illustrations only, 1982)

George's Marvelous Medicine (Illustrations only, 1981)

Mister Magnolia (1980)

Twits (Illustrations only, 1980)

Patrick (1968)

A Drink of Water and Other Stories (Illustrations only, 1960)

Blake's Major Literary Awards

2005 Boston Globe-Horn Book Nonfiction Honor Book
   Michael Rosen's Sad Book

2002 Hans Christian Andersen Award for Illustrators

1980 Kate Greenaway Medal
   Mister Magnolia

1976 Hans Christian Andersen Award for Illustrators

> *"I like drawing anything that is doing something. I like activity. Dragons are good because you can arrange them in interesting ways across the page, get people to ride on them, that sort of thing. Most animals are interesting to draw. Cars are difficult unless they are a bit broken down."*

though. By then, he had realized that he should use his artistic talent to illustrate stories. In 1958, he began studying at the Chelsea College of Art while submitting illustrations to *Punch*, *Spectator*, and other magazines.

Blake illustrated his first children's book—*A Drink of Water and Other Stories*—for author John Yeoman in 1960. Since then, he has created art for books by eighty different authors. But Blake is perhaps most famous for his illustrations in Roald Dahl's books, including classics such as *Charlie and the Chocolate Factory* and *James and the Giant Peach*. Blake has also illustrated books by Joan Aiken, Patrick Campbell, and Michael Rosen.

In 1968, Blake published *Patrick*, the first book he both wrote and illustrated. Many self-illustrated texts followed. Some of his popular and hilarious books include *Mister Magnolia*, *Mrs. Armitage on Wheels*, and *The Story of the Dancing Frog*.

Blake served as head of the Illustration Department at London's Royal College of Art from 1978 to 1986. After that, he devoted himself

BLAKE HAS ALSO ILLUSTRATED BOOKS WRITTEN BY SUCH BELOVED AUTHORS AS LEWIS CARROLL, JULES VERNE, RUDYARD KIPLING, CHARLES DICKENS, AND DR. SEUSS.

entirely to illustration. In 1988, he was named Officer to the Order of the British Empire for his service to children's literature. Blake was declared Great Britain's first children's laureate in 1999. As laureate, he traveled around the country promoting children's literature. He was named Commander of the Order of the British Empire in 2005, a rank just below knighthood.

Blake lives most of the year in London. He also spends time in Hastings, England, and southwestern France.

> *"I don't have children, but am still in touch with the child in me, and this has been immensely important to me as an artist. Part of keeping one's child-self alive is not being embarrassed to admit it exists."*

❧

WHERE TO FIND OUT MORE ABOUT QUENTIN BLAKE

BOOKS

Martin, Douglas. *The Telling Line: Essays on Fifteen Contemporary Book Illustrators.* London: Julia MacRae Books, 1989.

Silvey, Anita, ed. *The Essential Guide to Children's Books and Their Creators.* Boston: Houghton Mifflin Company, 2002.

WEB SITE
THE OFFICIAL QUENTIN BLAKE WEB SITE
http://www.quentinblake.com/
To find a biography, the latest news, downloads for children, and teacher tips

———

BLAKE BEGINS AN ILLUSTRATION WITH A PEN-AND-INK DRAWING. FOR SOME ILLUSTRATIONS, HE ADDS WATERCOLORS, WHILE OTHERS ARE LEFT AS BLACK-AND-WHITE ART.

Rhoda Blumberg

Born: December 14, 1917

History is not everyone's favorite subject. But anyone who reads Rhoda Blumberg's historical nonfiction books is sure to become a fan. She makes history truly exciting for young readers, giving them a behind-the-scenes glimpse into famous people and events from different eras.

Blumberg was born Rhoda Lois Shapiro in New York City in 1917. She graduated from Adelphi College in Garden City, New York, in 1938. She then pursued graduate studies at New York City's Columbia University.

From 1940 through 1944, she worked as a researcher and scriptwriter for CBS Radio in New York City. This gave her valuable experience in both researching and writing—skills that would serve her well in her later career as an author. In 1945, she switched to NBC Radio, where she worked as a talent scout. That same year, she married attorney Gerald Blumberg. The couple have four children—Lawrence,

---

BLUMBERG'S DAUGHTER, LEDA BLUMBERG, IS ALSO A CHILDREN'S BOOK AUTHOR.

Rena, Alice, and Leda. While Rhoda Blumberg raised her family, she worked as a freelance researcher for magazines until 1951.

In 1973, Blumberg decided to work in an office again. She took a job at Simon & Schuster publishing company, where she served as the executive editor of its Travel Guides series. Soon she began writing children's books. Her first book, *Firefighters*, was published in 1975. Over the next few years, Blumberg wrote several nonfiction books for young readers. She covered subjects as diverse as first ladies, sharks, witches, and UFOs.

> *"If monsters had descended upon Japan the effect could not have been more terrifying."*
> —*from* **Commodore Perry in the Land of the Shogun**

A great deal of science research went into Blumberg's *The First Travel Guide to the Moon* and *The First Travel Guide to the Bottom of the Sea*. But she would ultimately become best known for her historical nonfiction books. The first of these, *Commodore Perry in the Land of the Shogun*, was published in 1985. Again, Blumberg did meticulous research to bring her subject to life.

Sometimes Blumberg's research opened up a new area of interest for her. While she was doing research for *The Remarkable Voyages of Captain Cook*, she ran across information about a Japanese boy who was rescued from a shipwreck. She decided to write a separate book about this boy

---

MANJIRO NAKAHAMA IS THE HERO OF BLUMBERG'S BOOK *SHIPWRECKED!* HE SERVED AS A TRANSLATOR WHEN COMMODORE MATTHEW PERRY VISITED JAPAN IN 1853.

A Selected Bibliography of Blumberg's Work

York's Adventures with Lewis and Clark: An African-American's Part in the Great Expedition (2004)

Shipwrecked! The True Adventures of a Japanese Boy (2001)

Full Steam Ahead: The Race to Build a Transcontinental Railroad (1996)

Bloomers! (1993)

The Remarkable Voyages of Captain Cook (1991)

The Great American Gold Rush (1989)

The Incredible Journey of Lewis & Clark (1987)

Commodore Perry in the Land of the Shogun (1985)

The First Travel Guide to the Bottom of the Sea (1983)

Devils and Demons (1982)

The First Travel Guide to the Moon: What to Pack, How to Go, and What to See When You Get There (1980)

The Truth about Dragons (1980)

First Ladies (1977)

Firefighters (1975)

Blumberg's Major Literary Awards

2005 Orbis Pictus Award
York's Adventures with Lewis and Clark: An African-American's Part in the Great Expedition

1997 Orbis Pictus Honor Book
Full Steam Ahead: The Race to Build a Transcontinental Railroad

1990 Orbis Pictus Honor Book
The Great American Gold Rush

1986 Newbery Honor Book
1985 Boston Globe–Horn Book Nonfiction Award
Commodore Perry in the Land of the Shogun

and his amazing life. His story is told in *Shipwrecked! The True Adventures of a Japanese Boy*. Similarly, while Blumberg was working on *The Incredible Journey of Lewis & Clark*, she learned about William Clark's slave, York. That led Blumberg to write *York's Adventures with Lewis and Clark*.

Bloomers! recounts an interesting phase in the women's rights movement. It tells the story of Amelia Bloomer, who founded a women's newspaper in 1849.

"Imagine a boy of twelve or thirteen being the slave of a fourteen-year-old master!"
—*from* **York's Adventures with Lewis and Clark**

Bloomer was the first to publish illustrations of ladies wearing baggy trousers instead of dresses, and she encouraged women to place comfort and convenience before popular fashion. Her trousers, widely ridiculed at the time, eventually became known as bloomers.

Whether she is writing about exploration, discoveries, or cultural movements, Blumberg uses her literary talent to make nonfiction topics both informative and entertaining. She currently lives in Yorktown Heights, New York.

❧

WHERE TO FIND OUT MORE ABOUT RHODA BLUMBERG

BOOKS
Silvey, Anita, ed. *The Essential Guide to Children's Books and Their Creators.* Boston: Houghton Mifflin Company, 2002.

WEB SITES
HARPERCOLLINS
http://www.harperchildrens.com/authorintro/index.asp?authorid=15776
To read a biography about Rhoda Blumberg

INTERNET SCHOOL LIBRARY MEDIA CENTER
http://falcon.jmu.edu/~ramseyil/blumbergbib.htm
For a Rhoda Blumberg bibliography

BLUMBERG WAS AWARDED HER DEGREE FROM ADELPHI COLLEGE *MAGNA CUM LAUDE*, LATIN FOR "WITH GREAT DISTINCTION." STUDENTS MUST HAVE EXCEPTIONAL GRADES TO RECEIVE THIS HONOR.

Judy Blume

Born: February 12, 1938

As a child, Judy Blume dreamed of doing exciting things when she grew up. Being a writer was not one of them, however! Although she was always making up stories in her head, Judy did not think an ordinary person like herself could become a successful writer. "I made up stories while I bounced a ball against the side of our house. I made up stories playing with paper dolls. . . . I always had an active imagination. But I never wrote down any of my stories. And I never told anyone about them."

Blume was born on February 12, 1938, in Elizabeth, New Jersey. She was an involved student in school. In high school, she worked on the school newspaper, sang with the choir, and took part in school plays. She had lots of fun. Judy Blume remembers the teachers who made her think. After high school, she went to New York University to become a teacher. By the time she

---

BLUME'S DAUGHTER, RANDI, WROTE A BOOK CALLED *CRAZY IN THE COCKPIT* AND DEDICATED IT TO HER MOTHER.

graduated, she was married. She soon had two small children.

Although Blume enjoyed her time at home with her children, she knew she wanted to do something else. She started to think about writing books. Finally, she took a university course that taught how to write children's books. She liked it and took it again! Soon she was writing articles for magazines and had finished her first children's novel, *Iggie's House*. In 1970, Blume's third book, *Are You There God? It's Me, Margaret.* was published and became a huge success. Finally, Blume felt she was a real writer!

"Writing changed my life forever. It may have even saved it."

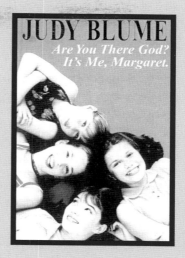

A Selected Bibliography of Blume's Work

Double Fudge (2002)
Here's to You, Rachel Robinson (1993)
The One in the Middle Is the Green Kangaroo (1991)
Fudge-a-Mania (1990)
Just As Long As We're Together (1987)
Superfudge (1980)
Starring Sally J. Freedman As Herself (1977)
Blubber (1974)
Deenie (1973)
Tales of a Fourth Grade Nothing (1972)
It's Not the End of the World (1972)
Otherwise Known As Sheila the Great (1972)
Then Again, Maybe I Won't (1971)
Freckle Juice (1971)
Are You There God? It's Me, Margaret. (1970)
Iggie's House (1970)
The One in the Middle Is the Green Kangaroo (1969)

Blume's books often deal with problems that real children face. Many of these problems are about sensitive or controversial issues for children. They include divorce, family breakups, friendships, and sexual issues. Some adults think Blume should not be writing about these subjects. But Blume believes it's important for children to have a way to deal with their feelings and questions about such subjects. "The way to instill values in children is to talk about difficult issues and bring them out in the open, not to restrict their access to books that may help them deal with their problems and concerns," she says.

> *"I wish that older readers would read my books about young people, and I hope that younger readers will grow up to read what I have to say about adult life."*

Children write to Judy Blume asking her questions and asking for advice. Blume says, "I have a wonderful, intimate relationship with kids. It's rare and lovely. They feel that they know me and that I know them." But Blume wishes that parents discussed issues more often with their children.

In fact, to encourage better communication between parents and their children, Blume has created the KIDS Fund. Blume donates some of the money she earns from the sale of her books to this fund. It gives money to organizations that help improve family communication.

BLUME CONSIDERS *STARRING SALLY J. FREEDMAN AS HERSELF*
THE MOST AUTOBIOGRAPHICAL OF HER BOOKS.

Blume's writing style is easy to read. She often writes in the first person, and her books read like journals or diaries. Her characters talk and think like real people. Blume says, "I have this gift, this memory, so it's easy to project myself back to certain stages in my life. And I write about what I know is true of kids going through those same stages."

> *"I'd like to feel that I write for everybody."*

Where to Find Out More about Judy Blume

Books

Marcus, Leonard S., ed. *Author Talk: Conversations with Judy Blume.* New York: Simon & Schuster, 2000.

McElmeel, Sharron L. *100 Most Popular Children's Authors: Biographical Sketches and Bibliographies.* Englewood, Colo.: Libraries Unlimited, 1999.

Weidt, Maryann N. *Presenting Judy Blume.* New York.: Twayne Publishers, 1990.

Wheeler, Jill C. *Judy Blume.* Edina, Minn.: Abdo and Daughters, 1996.

Web Sites

Judy Blume Home Page
http://www.judyblume.com
To read an autobiographical account, information on her books, writing tips from Blume, and her feelings on censorship

Teachers@Random: Authors and Illustrators
http://www.randomhouse.com/author/results.pperl?authorid=2611
To read a letter from Judy Blume and find answers to frequently asked questions about her life and books

TeenReads.com
http://www.teenreads.com/authors/au-blume-judy.asp
To read a short biographical sketch and an interview with the author

---

Blume went to an all-girls high school. It was the only one in the state of New Jersey!

Felicia Bond

Born: July 18, 1954

Felicia Bond tells a story about the moment when she decided to be an artist. She was a five-year-old living with her family in Bronxville, New York. "I was standing in the doorway of my bedroom in the late afternoon. The room was dark, except for a brilliant, but soft, beam of sunlight filtering through the window. At the base of the window was a red leather window seat, and it glowed a rich, dark color. I was moved somehow, and decided I had to capture that feeling of poignancy and time passing."

Born on July 18, 1954, Felicia Bond was one of seven children. She started to use her art as a way of standing out among her brothers and sisters. One day, a teacher who knew about Felicia's interest asked her to draw a mural for the class. She spread out a large sheet of butcher paper on the floor. The teacher asked Felicia to take off her shoes before she started to work so that she didn't smudge her work. Felicia was shy at first—she never took off her

---

ONE OF BOND'S FAVORITE ARTISTS WHEN SHE WAS A CHILD WAS CHARLES SCHULZ, WHO DREW THE COMIC STRIP *PEANUTS*. SHE LOVED THE PRECISE WAY HE BROUGHT OUT THE EXPRESSIONS ON HIS CHARACTERS' FACES. SHE ALSO LOVED THE MADELINE BOOKS.

shoes outside the house. But when she did, she was surprised at how free she felt. She says it was the first time she realized that artists didn't have to do what other people did.

Felicia Bond's family moved to Texas when she was thirteen. After high school, Bond went to the University of Texas at Austin, where she studied painting. When she graduated in 1976, she moved for a while to Edmonton in Alberta, Canada. She decided that she was interested in illustrations for children and set to work building a collection of work that she could show to editors.

> *"Some of my ideas spring forth full-grown, others sometimes gestate for years. I write down things in my sketchbook, which now has more words in it than drawings. I try to stay 'free-form' about my ideas so they don't become stiff or mechanical."*

Creating the illustrations took some time, so Bond took a series of jobs to pay the rent. Her jobs mostly involved art. She drew botanical illustrations for a science center in Houston. Then she did something she had wanted to do for many years: she moved back to New York. There she got jobs as a designer for several book publishers.

Finally, Bond got the chance to work on a children's book. Partly because of her experience in botany, she was hired to illustrate a science book called *When Birds Change Their Feathers*. Bond illustrated three

FOR A WHILE AFTER COLLEGE, BOND WORKED AS A PUPPETEER. SHE ADAPTED STORIES INTO PLAYS, DESIGNED AND MADE THE PUPPETS, AND PUT ON SHOWS FOR A PUBLIC LIBRARY IN HOUSTON, TEXAS.

A Selected Bibliography of Bond's Work

If You Give a Pig a Party (Illustrations only, 2005)

If You Take a Mouse to School (Illustrations only, 2002)

The Day It Rained Hearts (2002)

Little Porcupine's Christmas (Illustrations only, 2001)

If You Take a Mouse to the Movies (Illustrations only, 2000)

The Best Mouse Cookie (Illustrations only, 1999)

If You Give a Pig a Pancake (Illustrations only, 1998)

Tumble Bumble (1996)

Christmas in the Manger (Illustrations only, 1994)

The Big Green Pocketbook (Illustrations only, 1993)

If You Give a Moose a Muffin (Illustrations only, 1991)

The Right Number of Elephants (Illustrations only, 1990)

Big Red Barn (1989)

Wake Up, Vladimir (1987)

If You Give a Mouse a Cookie (Illustrations only, 1985)

Mama's Secret (Illustrations only, 1984)

Poinsettia and the Firefighters (1984)

Christmas in the Chicken Coop (1983)

Four Valentines in a Rainstorm (1983)

The Halloween Performance (1983)

The Halloween Play (1983)

Mary Betty Lizzie McNutt's Birthday (1983)

The Firelings (1982)

How Little Porcupine Played Christmas (1982)

Poinsettia & Her Family (1981)

The Sky Is Full of Stars (1981)

When Birds Change Their Feathers (1980)

more science books over the next few years.

Now Bond had an idea for a book of her own, a story about a little pig that thinks her house is too small and would be much nicer without her nine brothers and sisters. The book, *Poinsettia & Her Family,* was published in 1981 and was chosen best book of the year by *School Library Journal.* Bond continued writing books of her own, including *Four Valentines in a Rainstorm, Wake Up, Vladimir,* and *Tumble Bumble.* She also continued illustrating books by other authors.

In 1985, one of those illustration projects became a big success. Bond worked with writer Laura Numeroff on a book called *If You Give a Mouse a Cookie.* The idea was humorous but simple—if you give a mouse a cookie, he'll want some milk to go with it. If you give him milk, he'll want a straw, and so on and so on. Bond's lively, funny pictures helped the book become a best seller. Other titles soon followed: *If You Give a Moose a Muffin, If You Take a Mouse to the Movies* (he'll want popcorn, of course), and even a mouse cookie cookbook.

Felicia Bond lives in Austin, Texas. She is currently working on several new books.

> *"[I]n 1980, I wrote Poinsettia & Her Family. I couldn't believe how hard it was to see the book through to completion. My entire life came to a halt as I executed it. Nor could I believe how good I felt when it was finished."*

WHERE TO FIND OUT MORE ABOUT FELICIA BOND

BOOK
Silvey, Anita, ed. *The Essential Guide to Children's Books and Their Creators.* Boston: Houghton Mifflin Company, 2002.

WEB SITES
FELICIA BOND HOME PAGE
feliciabondbooks.com
To read a biography, to see the book covers, and to read excerpts from her books

MEET THE ILLUSTRATOR: FELICIA BOND
http://www.eduplace.com/kids/hmr/mtai/bond.html
To read a biography and booklist for Felicia Bond

BOND TOOK A LONG TIME TO DRAW THE PIG IN *IF YOU GIVE A PIG A PANCAKE.* "I DREW DOZENS OF PIGS. DOZENS. AT LEAST THIRTY," SHE SAYS. "AND IT WASN'T UNTIL SIX MONTHS INTO DESIGNING THE BOOK THAT I REALIZED I DIDN'T WANT HER TO BE A TYPICAL CHUNKY PINK PIG, AND I ADDED SOME FUZZ AND A FEW SPOTS."

Michael Bond

Born: January 13, 1926

Michael Bond was not a very famous writer until he met a stuffed Peruvian bear around Christmastime 1957. The bear was the last one on the shelves of a store near his home in London, England, and Bond felt a little sorry for the lonely bear.

He bought him as a gift for his wife and named him Paddington after the train station down the street.

Rescued from the uneventful life of an unwanted toy, Paddington Bear decided to repay Michael Bond by giving him the idea for a series of children's stories. The hero of the stories—Paddington Bear himself— likes to repay one good turn with another. He is a good-hearted bear,

---

MICHAEL BOND AND HIS DAUGHTER, KAREN, HAVE WRITTEN SEVERAL PADDINGTON BEAR BOOKS TOGETHER, INCLUDING *PADDINGTON GOES TO THE HOSPITAL*, *PADDINGTON'S FIRST PUZZLE BOOK*, AND *PADDINGTON MAILS A LETTER*.

and he has helped no one as much as Michael Bond.

Bond was born in Newbury, England, on January 13, 1926, and grew up in the English town of Reading. Like Paddington Bear, he never took life too seriously. He found good company in animals. He spent time catching newts and playing with guinea pigs and his dog, Binkie. When Michael was a child, his world was safe and interesting. One could have adventures and misadventures and still end up all right. This is now the world of Paddington Bear.

> *"When Paddington goes back home, it's the world that I remember from my childhood."*

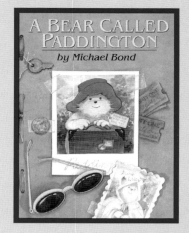

A Selected Bibliography of Bond's Work

Paddington Bear in the Garden (2002)
Paddington at Work (2001)
Paddington Goes to the Hospital (2001)
Paddington's Party Tricks (2000)
Paddington and the Marmalade Maze (1999)
Paddington Treasury (1999)
Paddington Bear All Day (1998)
Paddington's Things I Feel (1994)
Paddington's First Word Book (1993)
Paddington's ABC (1990)
Paddington's First Puzzle Book (1987)
Paddington's Busy Day (1987)
The Hilarious Adventures of Paddington (1986)
Paddington Mails a Letter (1986)
Paddington Takes the Test (1980)
Paddington at the Circus (1974)
Paddington Bear (1973)
The Tales of Olga da Polga (1973)
Thursday Ahoy! (1970)
Paddington Goes to Town (1969)
Here Comes Thursday (1967)
Paddington Marches On (1965)
Paddington at Large (1963)
More about Paddington (1962)
Paddington Helps Out (1961)
A Bear Called Paddington (1960)

Bond started to write during World War II (1939– 1945). He joined the Royal Air Force in 1943, working as a navigator. He found the air force interesting, but got airsick when he was flying. That made him unsuitable for the air force, so he transferred to the British army. He was stationed in the Middle East where he spent his time "picking stones out of the desert." To pass the time, he began to write stories and plays. This was his start as a writer. Sometimes magazines published his work, and sometimes he sold plays to be read over the radio.

> *"If an author doesn't believe in his inventions and his characters nobody else will. Paddington to me is, and always has been, very much alive."*

After he left the army, Bond became a full-time writer in England and married Brenda Mary Johnson. Bond tried to make a living from writing and part-time work at the British Broadcasting Corporation (BBC). Most years, he didn't make much money, but his imagination kept him going.

In 1958, his wife gave birth to their daughter, Karen. That same year another creation came to life—*A Bear Called Paddington.* Paddington was drawn by the illustrator Peggy Fortnum. She drew him with his duffel coat, rain boots, and floppy hat. Although others illustrated later Paddington Bear books, these trademarks make Paddington easily recognizable.

———

MICHAEL BOND WRITES FOR ADULTS, TOO. HE CREATED A FRENCH DETECTIVE NAMED MONSIEUR PAMPLEMOUSSE, WHO SOLVES CRIME WITH THE HELP OF HIS DOG, POMMES FRITES, WHICH MEANS "FRENCH FRIES" IN ENGLISH.

Michael Bond has written about other animals, too. Olga da Polga is a guinea pig, and Thursday is a mouse. They both have their own series of books. These animals all have the characteristics of people and live in an eventful and imaginative world. But it is Paddington that has given Michael Bond a way to re-create the cozy world of his childhood in England.

∾

WHERE TO FIND OUT MORE ABOUT MICHAEL BOND

BOOKS

Collier, Laurie, and Joyce Nakamura, eds. *Major Authors and Illustrators for Children and Young Adults: A Selection of Sketches from Something about the Author.* Detroit: Gale Research, 1993.

McElmeel, Sharron L. *100 Most Popular Children's Authors: Biographical Sketches and Bibliographies.* Englewood, Colo.: Libraries Unlimited, 1999.

Silvey, Anita, ed. *The Essential Guide to Children's Books and Their Creators.* Boston: Houghton Mifflin Company, 2002.

WEB SITES

MEET PADDINGTON BEAR AND HIS CREATORS
http://www.harperchildrens.com/hch/author/author/bond
To read information on Michael Bond and an interview with Paddington

PADDINGTON BEAR—THE OFFICIAL WEB SITE
www.paddingtonbear.co.uk
To read information about Paddington Bear and how
he was created, as well as to play online games

———

IN 1997, MICHAEL BOND WAS AWARDED THE ORDER OF THE BRITISH EMPIRE FOR SERVICES TO CHILDREN'S LITERATURE. THE AWARD, CREATED IN 1917 DURING WORLD WAR I (1914–1918) BY KING GEORGE V, IS GIVEN FOR CONTRIBUTIONS TO VARIOUS ASPECTS OF BRITISH LIFE.

Aliki Brandenberg

Born: September 3, 1929

liki uses only her first name on her books. Her full name is Aliki Liacouras Brandenberg. She was born on September 3, 1929, in Wildwood Crest, New Jersey. Wildwood Crest is a seashore resort where her family was vacationing when she was born. The family lived in Philadelphia. Her parents were from Greece. As a child, Aliki spoke Greek before she spoke English.

Aliki began to draw as a young child. She remembers that two of her paintings were exhibited when she was in kindergarten. They were portraits of families with three girls and a youngster named Peter. The portrait of the three girls represented her family. The other portrait was Peter Rabbit's family! She thinks her choice of career was decided there and then by the attention the two paintings received.

ALIKI'S WORK HAS WON AWARDS FROM MANY ORGANIZATIONS, INCLUDING THE BOYS CLUBS OF AMERICA, THE NEW JERSEY INSTITUTE OF TECHNOLOGY, AND THE NEW YORK ACADEMY OF SCIENCES.

While she was in school, Aliki took Saturday art classes. After high school, she attended the Philadelphia Museum College of Art and graduated in 1951. For a year, she worked in the display department of the J. C. Penney Company. Then she worked in advertising and art display. She painted murals and taught art and ceramics. She even had a greeting-card company.

On a 1956 trip to Italy and Greece, Aliki took a special interest in her Greek heritage. On that trip, she also met her husband, Franz Brandenberg. After their marriage, they lived in Switzerland.

Aliki and her husband visited the area in Switzerland where William Tell had lived. She wrote her first book about the legend of the Swiss hero who helped his country fight an Austrian invasion. An Austrian official ordered William Tell to shoot an apple off his son's head with an arrow. Tell's first arrow hit the apple and spared his son. *The Story of William Tell* was published in England in 1960.

In 1960, the Brandenbergs moved to New York. Their two children, Jason and Alexa, were born in the 1960s. Aliki was asked to illustrate several books. While she worked, Aliki had an idea for another book she wanted to write. It was *My Five Senses.* She wrote it—and

"I have always felt close to children and books, and feel fortunate that I can direct what creativity I have to both."

ALIKI GETS STORY IDEAS FROM HER OWN EXPERIENCES, THOSE OF HER SON AND DAUGHTER, AND EVEN THOSE OF HER NEIGHBORS. *AT MARY BLOOM'S* IS ABOUT HER DAUGHTER'S VISIT TO A NEIGHBOR.

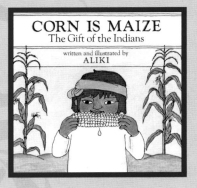

A Selected Bibliography of Aliki's Work

Play's the Thing (2005)
Ah, Music! (2002)
One Little Spoonful (2001)
All by Myself (2000)
William Shakespeare and the Globe (1999)
Painted Words; Spoken Memories (1998)
My Visit to the Zoo (1997)
Hello! Good-bye! (1996)
The Gods and Goddesses of Olympus (1994)
The Big Book for Our Planet (1993)
Communication (1993)
I'm Growing! (1992)
Milk: From Cow to Carton (1992)
Evolution (Illustrations only, 1987)
How a Book Is Made (1986)
Dinosaurs Are Different (1985)
Feelings (1984)
A Medieval Feast (1983)
We Are Best Friends (1982)
Digging Up Dinosaurs (1981)
It's Not My Fault (Illustrations only, 1980)
Mummies Made in Egypt (1979)
At Mary Bloom's (1976)
Corn Is Maize: The Gift of the Indians (1976)
Diogenes: The Story of the Greek Philosopher (1968)
My Five Senses (1962)
The Story of William Tell (1961)

Aliki's Major Literary Award

1999 Boston Globe-Horn Book Nonfiction Honor Book
    William Shakespeare and the Globe

illustrated it—in five days! Future books did not come that quickly, though.

Aliki is an artist, first and foremost. Her art takes many forms. Sometimes she draws simple shapes and uses bright colors. Other times she makes whimsical sketches and old-fashioned drawings that tell a story. For *How a Book Is Made,* she developed a comic-book style. She has illustrated fifteen books of her own and more than fifty books written by other authors, including her husband, Franz Brandenberg.

Aliki's work includes both fiction and nonfiction. She likes to research complicated science and history subjects and write about them in a simple, straightforward way for young readers. She also tries to write with humor when possible. Aliki has written about Benjamin Franklin, George Washington, George Washington Carver, and others. She has also translated Greek folktales and written about the Greek philosopher Diogenes.

Aliki and her family moved to England in the late 1970s. She continues her work as an illustrator and author, publishing and illustrating several books each year.

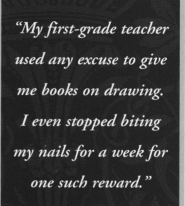

"My first-grade teacher used any excuse to give me books on drawing. I even stopped biting my nails for a week for one such reward."

WHERE TO FIND OUT MORE ABOUT ALIKI

BOOKS
Kovacs, Deborah, and James Preller. *Meet the Authors and Illustrators: 60 Creators of Favorite Children's Books Talk about Their Work.* Vol. 2. New York: Scholastic, 1993.

McElmeel, Sharron L. *100 Most Popular Picture Book Authors and Illustrators: Biographical Sketches and Bibliographies.* Englewood, Colo.: Libraries Unlimited, 2000.

Silvey, Anita, ed. *Children's Books and Their Creators.* Boston: Houghton Mifflin, 1995.

WEB SITE
ALIKIBOOKS.COM
To read a biography of Aliki, autobiographical thoughts and notes, and to see her book covers and sample chapters

ALIKI BELIEVES THAT IDEAS FOR BOOKS DEVELOP SLOWLY IN HER MIND AND ARE RELEASED BY A PEN AND A CLEAN SHEET OF PAPER.

Jan Brett

Born: December 1, 1949

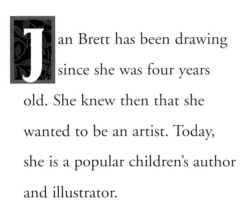

Jan Brett has been drawing since she was four years old. She knew then that she wanted to be an artist. Today, she is a popular children's author and illustrator.

Jan Brett was born on December 1, 1949, in Hingham, Massachusetts. As a child, Jan did not find it easy to express her feelings in words. Instead, she drew pictures. Jan loved to spend her time drawing and reading. "I remember the special quiet of rainy days, when I felt that I could enter the pages of beautiful picture books," she says. Jan's parents and friends encouraged her to continue drawing.

BRETT'S FAVORITE ANIMAL TO DRAW IS A HORSE. SHE'S BEEN DRAWING HORSES SINCE SHE WAS IN FIRST GRADE.

Brett went to the Boston Museum of Fine Arts School. She spent many hours in the Museum of Fine Arts. She studied the art that was there. Brett memorized many of the details of the large paintings and tapestries.

After that, she worked as a painter and then as a children's book illustrator. Her first book of illustrations was *Woodland Crossings,* published in 1978. Brett didn't intend to write her own stories. Then a publisher convinced her to try. *Fritz and the Beautiful Horses,* the first book Brett wrote and illustrated, was published in 1981. She still enjoys illustrating books most of all. But writing is also important to her. "The hardest thing

A Selected Bibliography of Brett's Work

Hedgie Blasts Off (2006)
Umbrella (2004)
On Noah's Ark (2003)
Daisy Comes Home (2002)
Who's That Knocking on Christmas Eve? (2002)
Jan Brett's Christmas Treasury (2001)
Hedgie's Surprise (2000)
Gingerbread Baby (1999)
The Hat (1997)
Armadillo Rodeo (1995)
Town Mouse, Country Mouse (1994)
Christmas Trolls (1993)
Trouble with Trolls (1992)
Berlioz the Bear (1991)
The Wild Christmas Reindeer (1990)
The Mitten: A Ukrainian Folktale (1989)
The First Dog (1988)
Goldilocks and the Three Bears (1987)
The Twelve Days of Christmas (Illustrations only, 1986)
Annie and the Wild Animals (1985)
Fritz and the Beautiful Horses (1981)
St. Patrick's Day in the Morning (Illustrations only, 1980)
Woodland Crossings (Illustrations only, 1978)

about a book is not the subject and not the setting, but the plot—what happens in the story. Usually, I have to start from the plot," Brett notes.

Today, Brett uses the details she still remembers from her time at the Museum of Fine Arts. It is important to her to use detail in her illustrations.

> *"Take a little time out to write a story—because stories are like a little fingerprint. No one can write a story just like you."*

She gets ideas from the world around her. She believes it is the details that help make the story seem real. "I try to get a feel for the country and times my characters live in, and I get many ideas from traveling to different countries, where I research the architecture and costumes that appear in my work," Brett explains.

Many of Brett's illustrations have borders on the pages that add interest and information to the story. *Annie and the Wild Animals* was the first book that included her beautiful borders. Brett has said that the book that best represents her style is *Trouble with Trolls*. It is a story about a young girl, her dog, some trolls—and a hedgehog! (Brett has a hedgehog for a pet.)

Brett gets her story and illustration ideas from her memories, from daydreaming, and from her travels. She wrote three books after a trip to Norway. Her books continue to be popular with children and

AS A CHILD, BRETT'S FAVORITE CHILDREN'S BOOK
WAS *MILLIONS OF CATS* BY WANDA GÁG.

adults. They have also been published in many languages.

Today, Jan Brett continues to write and illustrate children's books. She lives near the coast of Massachusetts with her family.

> *"I can't communicate my ideas any other way as well as when I'm drawing."*

❧

WHERE TO FIND OUT MORE ABOUT JAN BRETT

BOOKS

Kovacs, Deborah, and James Preller. *Meet the Authors and Illustrators: 60 Creators of Favorite Children's Books Talk about Their Work.* Vol. 2. New York: Scholastic, 1993.

McElmeel, Sharron L. *100 Most Popular Picture Book Authors and Illustrators: Biographical Sketches and Bibliographies.* Englewood, Colo.: Libraries Unlimited, 2000.

Silvey, Anita, ed. *The Essentail Guide to Children's Books and Their Creators.* Boston: Houghton Mifflin, 2002.

WEB SITE

JAN BRETT HOME PAGE
http://www.janbrett.com/
To read autobiographical information, work on activity pages, and view a booklist

IT'S HARD FOR BRETT TO FINISH A BOOK BECAUSE SHE DOESN'T WANT IT TO END. SHE FALLS IN LOVE WITH THE CHARACTERS, SO FINISHING WORK ON A BOOK IS LIKE SAYING GOOD-BYE TO THEM.

Norman Bridwell

Born: February 15, 1928

One of the best-known animals in children's literature is Clifford the Big Red Dog. Clifford was created by illustrator and writer Norman Bridwell. This popular animal has been featured in forty-two of the more than sixty books Bridwell has published during his long career.

Bridwell was born on February 15, 1928, in Kokomo, Indiana. He began drawing as a young boy. His father worked in a factory and brought home used order forms. Norman used the back of the forms for his drawings.

Walking to and from school, Norman used his imagination to create many stories. He never wrote any of the stories down on paper,

———

WHEN HE CREATED A BIG RED DOG FOR HIS FIRST CHILDREN'S BOOK, BRIDWELL WANTED TO NAME THE DOG TINY. INSTEAD, HIS WIFE SUGGESTED THE NAME CLIFFORD, WHICH WAS THE NAME OF HER IMAGINARY CHILDHOOD FRIEND.

but he drew pictures to go with the stories. "I always liked to draw," Bridwell notes, "but I was never considered very good." His art teacher at school never thought Bridwell's drawings were anything special.

After graduating from high school, Bridwell knew he wanted to try to work as an illustrator. He enrolled in a four-year art school in Indianapolis to study drawing. When he finished his studies at the art school, he was not able to find a job as an artist in Indiana. He moved to New York City and took classes at another art school for two more years. He then began working as an artist.

> *"Clifford does what you'd like to do but can't. Because Clifford is so big and also because he's a dog, he's able to do the most unbelievable and imaginative things."*

Bridwell took many jobs to earn money. He worked as a messenger, designed men's neckties, and drew cartoons for filmstrips and slide shows. In 1962, Bridwell had a hard time finding work. He decided to try to find a job as a children's book illustrator. After he put together a collection of his drawings, Bridwell visited more than fifteen publishing companies. No one offered him any work.

An editor at one publishing company suggested that Bridwell write a story to go along with one of his drawings. Bridwell selected a drawing of a small girl and a large dog. He worked quickly to write the text and

---

WHEN BRIDWELL HAD TO NAME HIS CHARACTERS IN THE FIRST CLIFFORD BOOK, THE NAME OF THE LITTLE GIRL WAS EASY TO CHOOSE. HE NAMED THE CHARACTER EMILY ELIZABETH, AFTER HIS OWN YOUNG DAUGHTER.

A Selected Bibliography of Bridwell's Work

Clifford's First Sleepover (2004)
Clifford Goes to Dog School (2002)
Clifford's Happy Mother's Day (2001)
Clifford's Valentines (2001)
The Cat and the Bird in the Hat (2000)
Clifford Barks (2000)
Clifford Visits the Hospital (2000)
Oops, Clifford! (1999)
Clifford and the Halloween Parade (1999)
Clifford Grows Up (1999)
Clifford and the Big Parade (1998)
Clifford's First Autumn (1997)
Clifford's Furry Friends (1996)
Clifford and the Big Storm (1995)
Clifford the Firehouse Dog (1994)
Clifford's Happy Easter (1994)
Clifford's Thanksgiving Visit (1993)
Clifford Follows His Nose (1992)
Clifford's Bedtime (1991)
Clifford's Birthday Party (1988)
Clifford and the Grouchy Neighbors (1985)
Clifford at the Circus (1985)
Clifford's Good Deeds (1975)
Clifford's Halloween (1966)
The Witch Next Door (1965)
Clifford the Big Red Dog (1963)

finish the illustrations. Three weeks after he delivered the sample book to the editor, the publishing company informed him they would be publishing *Clifford the Big Red Dog.*

Bridwell is much more comfortable as an illustrator than as a writer. "Doing the drawings is easy for me, but writing the words is not easy," Bridwell explains. It usually takes Bridwell about three months to complete the drawings and story for a book. He did one of his books very fast, though. Bridwell completed his book *The Witch Next Door* in about one day!

Today, more than 44 million copies of Bridwell's books are in print. Many of his books have been translated into several languages. He continues to write and illustrate books from his home in Martha's Vineyard, Massachusetts.

"I was not good at sports and my high school shop teacher, after a few days of class, took my tools away, telling me, 'Here's a pad of paper instead. You seem to like to draw: stick to that!' "

WHERE TO FIND OUT MORE ABOUT NORMAN BRIDWELL

BOOKS

Collier, Laurie, and Joyce Nakamura, eds. *Major Authors and Illustrators for Children and Young Adults: A Selection of Sketches from Something about the Author.* Detroit: Gale Research, 1993.

Holtze, Sally Holmes, ed. *Seventh Book of Junior Authors & Illustrators.* New York: H. W. Wilson Company, 1996.

McElmeel, Sharron L. *100 Most Popular Picture Book Authors and Illustrators: Biographical Sketches and Bibliographies.* Englewood, Colo.: Libraries Unlimited, 2000.

Silvey, Anita, ed. *The Essential Guide to Children's Books and Their Creators.* Boston: Houghton Mifflin Company, 2002.

WEB SITES

CLIFFORD THE BIG RED DOG
http://pbskids.org/clifford/
For frequently asked questions about Clifford, games, and printable coloring pages

EDUCATIONAL PAPERBACK ASSOCIATION
http://www.edupaperback.org/showauth.cfm?authid=236
For autobiographical information and a booklist

BRIDWELL DECIDED MANY YEARS AGO THAT CLIFFORD WOULD NEVER DO ANYTHING IN THE BOOKS THAT A REAL DOG WOULD NOT DO.

Walter Brooks

Born: January 9, 1886
Died: August 17, 1958

He's a detective, he's a pilot, he's a magician—he's Freddy the Pig! Thousands of kids in the 1940s and 1950s grew up reading about Freddy and his barnyard friends. But Freddy gave kids more than just entertainment. He taught them lessons in resourcefulness, loyalty, and ethics. This versatile porker is the creation of author Walter Brooks. Brooks wrote twenty-six Freddy volumes between 1927 and 1958.

Walter Rollin Brooks was born in Rome, New York, in 1886. His father, a music teacher, died when Walter was only four. Walter's mother died when he was fifteen.

In 1902, Walter enrolled in Mohegan Lake Military Academy in Peekskill, New York. Then in 1904, he went to live with his older sister, Elsie, in Rochester, New York. There he attended the University of Rochester for two years. Elsie's husband was a doctor of homeopathic medicine, and through him, Walter

---

THE FRIENDS OF FREDDY IS AN ORGANIZATION FOUNDED IN 1984 TO CELEBRATE FREDDY THE PIG AND PRESERVE THE WRITINGS OF WALTER BROOKS.

gained an interest in that field. (Homeopathy is a form of alternative medicine that gained popularity in the United States in the late 1800s.) Walter moved to New York City, where he began classes at the Homeopathic Medical College in 1906. But he dropped out in 1908 and moved back to Rochester. In 1909, he married Anne Mary Shepard, a schoolteacher and artist.

Brooks enjoyed writing, and his first published works appeared in magazines in 1915. One was a poem, and the other was a short story for adults. From 1917 to 1927, Brooks did most of his writing as a publicist for the American Red Cross. Freddy the Pig made his debut in Brooks's first children's

A Selected Bibliography of Brooks's Work

Freddy and the Dragon (1958)
Freddy and Simon the Dictator (1956)
Freddy and the Baseball Team from Mars (1955)
Freddy and the Space Ship (1953)
The Collected Poems of Freddy the Pig (1953)
Freddy and Freginald (1952)
Freddy the Cowboy (1950)
Freddy Goes to Florida (1949)
Freddy Plays Football (1949)
Freddy the Explorer (1949)
Freddy the Politician (1948)
Freddy the Magician (1947)
Freddy and the Bean Home News (1943)
The Clockwork Twin (1937)
Freddy the Detective (1932)
To and Again (1927)

> *"Freddy . . . knew how to read, and he had gathered together quite a library of the books and magazines and newspapers that different animals had brought in. . . . He kept them in a corner of the pig-pen which he called his study."*
> —from **Freddy the Detective**

book, *To and Again*, in 1927. (This book was republished in 1949 as *Freddy Goes to Florida*.) Freddy is introduced as "the smallest and cleverest of the pigs" on Mr. Bean's farm.

From 1928 until 1940, Brooks worked as an editor and writer for several New York magazines. He also continued writing short stories, mostly for *Esquire* magazine. Some of his stories star Ed, a talking horse. That character became the basis for the 1960s TV series *Mister Ed*. But what brought Brooks the most fame was his collection of Freddy stories.

These books were quite unusual in their day. Most children's literature at that time portrayed animals in their traditional roles as cuddly pets or fascinating examples of nature. Freddy, however, is quite an activist. He fights corruption and foils a number of villains, from sneaky robbers to greedy bank presidents to corrupt business tycoons.

> *"Some of the dudes began to giggle and make remarks behind their hands, for while as a pig Freddy was nothing to laugh at, as a cowboy he really was sort of funny looking."*
> —from **Freddy the Cowboy**

BROOKS'S HOMETOWN OF ROME, NEW YORK, IS BELIEVED TO BE THE MODEL FOR CENTERBORO, FREDDY THE PIG'S HOMETOWN.

Freddy often has a big mystery to solve. To do so, he sometimes becomes a detective and works in disguise. Or he may put his Animal Bureau of Investigation (ABI) into action. Freddy has a poetic side, too. He wrote so many poems that they were published in 1953 as *The Collected Poems of Freddy the Pig*.

Brooks's wife, Anne, died in 1952, and he married Dorothy Collins later that same year. Brooks died in 1958 in Roxbury, New York.

WHERE TO FIND OUT MORE ABOUT WALTER BROOKS

BOOKS

Almanac of Famous People. 7th ed. Detroit, Mich.: Gale, 2000.

Pendergast, Sara, and Tom Pendergast, eds. *St. James Guide to Children's Writers*. 5th ed. Detroit: St. James Press, 1999.

Silvey, Anita, ed. *The Essential Guide to Children's Books and Their Creators*. Boston: Houghton Mifflin Company, 2002.

WEB SITES

FREDDY THE PIG
http://www.freddythepig.org/brooks.html
For a biography, pictures, news, and Freddy's Store

KIDS READS
http://www.kidsreads.com/series/series-freddy-reviews.asp
For book reviews of several Freddy books

ILLUSTRATOR KURT WIESE CREATED FREDDY THE PIG'S TRADEMARK LOOK AND ILLUSTRATED MOST OF BROOKS'S FREDDY BOOKS.

Marc Brown

Born: November 25, 1946

Marc Brown loves to draw. When he was young, he spent many hours with pens and paper. He knew he wanted to be an artist, and his grandmother encouraged him to draw. In time, he became interested in painting, too. In high school, his art teacher encouraged his interest in art and taught him to use watercolors.

Brown was born on November 25, 1946, in Erie, Pennsylvania. Originally his first name was spelled "Mark," but he later changed the

spelling to "Marc" as a tribute to the famous artist Marc Chagall. As a child, Marc spent a lot of time with his grandmother. "Our grandma Thora told us the most wonderful stories. Back then I never dreamed I would grow up to tell stories of my own," Brown remembers. After high school, Marc's parents were not excited that he wanted to study art. His grandma helped him decide to go to art school.

————

BROWN BASED *ARTHUR'S BABY* ON HIS OWN EXPERIENCES WITH HIS NEW BABY.

At the Cleveland Institute of Art, Marc Brown studied many art forms. He became interested in book illustrations. After finishing at Cleveland, Brown showed some of his illustrations to a publishing company. They hired him to make drawings for textbooks. These drawings had to match the text, however. Brown wanted more freedom to use his creativity in his illustrations.

In 1970, Brown was hired to illustrate a children's story by the science fiction and nonfiction author Isaac Asimov. It was called *What Makes the Sun Shine?* "I was a little nervous because Asimov was so famous. . . . After the book was done, he wrote saying that at

A Selected Bibliography of Brown's Work

Arthur's Back-to-School Fib (2007)
Arthur Loses a Friend (2006)
Buster and the Giant Pumpkin (2005)
D. W.'s Perfect Present (2004)
Arthur Tricks the Tooth Fairy (2003)
Arthur's Back-to-School Surprise (2002)
Arthur's First Kiss (2001)
Arthur's Fire Drill (2000)
Arthur's Lost Puppy (2000)
Arthur in a Pickle (1999)
Rex and Lilly School Time (1997)
Scared Silly! A Book for the Brave (1994)
Arthur's New Puppy (1993)
Arthur Meets the President (1991)
Arthur's Birthday (1989)
Arthur's Baby (1987)
Dinosaurs Divorce (1986)
Visiting the Art Museum (1986)
The Bionic Bunny Show (1984)
Dinosaurs Beware! A Safety Guide (1982)
The True Francine (1981)
Arthur's Eyes (1979)
Why the Tides Ebb and Flow (Illustrations only, 1979)
Arthur's Nose (1976)
What Makes the Sun Shine? (Illustrations only, 1970)

Brown's Major Literary Award

1980 Boston Globe–Horn Book Picture Book Honor Book
Why the Tides Ebb and Flow

first he wasn't sure about the artwork, until he looked through the eyes of a six-year-old child. Then he enjoyed it very much. I think that was a compliment," says Brown.

> *"Children must sense the great respect I have for them; that's how I explain the success of my books."*

Brown continued to illustrate other people's stories. At night, he told his own stories to his young son, Tolon. Many of these stories were about animals. One story was about an aardvark who hated his long nose. The aardvark's name was Arthur. Few children today do not know Arthur, D. W., Francine, and their friends.

Brown's characters are often based on people he has known. Grandma Thora in the Arthur books is based on his beloved grandmother. Mr. Ratburn is based on a mean algebra teacher Brown once had. His sisters and his own children have also given him ideas for characters.

Although Brown was an artist before he was a writer, the story is as important to him as the pictures. "When I develop books, I'm careful that the words and pictures are balanced. I think the best children's books work well for adults, too. If there isn't a good story line and some strong psychological ballast, it probably won't have much to offer children, either," Brown explains.

BEFORE BECOMING A FULL-TIME ILLUSTRATOR AND AUTHOR, BROWN HAD MANY JOBS. HE HAS WORKED AS A COLLEGE PROFESSOR, A CHICKEN FARMER, AND A TRUCK DRIVER!

Brown continues to write and illustrate children's stories. He also spends time each year traveling to schools. He enjoys talking to children about Arthur and the process

> *"I think of my work as telling stories in words and pictures."*

of making a book. Brown lives with his family in Hingham, Massachusetts, and in Martha's Vineyard, Massachusetts.

⌘

WHERE TO FIND OUT MORE ABOUT MARC BROWN

BOOKS

McElmeel, Sharron L. *100 Most Popular Picture Book Authors and Illustrators: Biographical Sketches and Bibliographies.* Englewood, Colo.: Libraries Unlimited, 2000.

Silvey, Anita, ed. *The Essential Guide to Children's Books and Their Creators.* Boston: Houghton Mifflin Company, 2002.

Woods, Mae. *Marc Brown.* Edina, Minn.: Abdo and Daughters, 2001.

WEB SITES

EDUCATIONAL PAPERBACK ASSOCIATION
http://edupaperback.org/showauth.cfm?authid=16
For an autobiographical account by Marc Brown and a selection of his book titles

PBS KIDS: ARTHUR
http://pbskids.org/arthur/
For biographical information, games, and descriptions of the characters in the Arthur series

———

BROWN'S WIFE, LAURIE KRASNY BROWN, ALSO WRITES CHILDREN'S BOOKS. THEY HAVE WORKED TOGETHER ON SEVERAL BOOKS.

Marcia Brown

Born: July 13, 1918

Even as a child, Marcia Brown knew she wanted to illustrate children's books. In particular, she wanted to illustrate ones for younger children. These books, she felt, had much better pictures than those for older kids. Brown accomplished her goal— she has illustrated more than thirty picture books for children.

Marcia Joan Brown was born in Rochester, New York, in 1918. She and her two sisters loved to read and draw. Marcia's favorite books were fairy tales by Hans Christian Andersen, the Brothers Grimm, and Charles Perrault, as well as the *Arabian Nights*. As she read, her mind filled with pictures, and she was constantly drawing.

When it was time for Brown to go to college, the country was in the midst of the Great Depression. Money was tight, and getting a job was a

---

MANY OF BROWN'S BOOKS HAVE BEEN PUBLISHED IN OTHER LANGUAGES, INCLUDING SPANISH, GERMAN, JAPANESE, AND SOUTH AFRICA'S AFRIKAANS AND XHOSA LANGUAGES.

priority. Even though she dreamed of being an illustrator, she had to make practical plans. So she decided to become a teacher. In 1936, Brown enrolled in New York State College for Teachers in Albany, New York. She majored in English and drama, and many of her humorous sketches were published in the school newspaper. She also designed sets and painted scenery for college plays.

"[T]he heritage of childhood is the sense of life bequeathed to it by the folk wisdom of the ages. To tell in pictures, to tell in words . . . it is a privilege to pass these truths on to children who have a right to the fullest expression we can give them."

After graduation in 1940, Brown taught high-school English and drama in Cornwall, New York. Then she made the big decision to follow her artistic dreams. She quit her teaching job in 1943 and moved to New York City. There she studied painting at the New School for Social Research. Meanwhile, she worked as a children's librarian at the New York Public Library. Interacting with kids at the library helped her develop ideas about good storytelling.

In New York City, Brown lived in an apartment in Greenwich Village. From her apartment window, she could see a carousel and the people who came to ride it. This led her to write and illustrate her first book, *The Little Carousel*, in 1946. The book did well, and this success gave Brown the courage to write more. Her first illustrated folk story was

MUCH OF BROWN'S ARTWORK IS HOUSED IN THE M. E. GRENANDER DEPARTMENT OF SPECIAL COLLECTIONS AND ARCHIVES AT THE UNIVERSITY OF ALBANY IN NEW YORK.

A Selected Bibliography of Brown's Work

Dick Whittington and His Cat (1997)

How the Ostrich Got Its Long Neck: A Tale from the Akamba of Kenya (1995)

Shadow (1982)

Walk with Your Eyes (1979)

All Butterflies (1974)

Backbone of the King: The Story of Paka'a and His Son Ku (1966)

Once a Mouse (1961)

Cinderella (1954)

The Steadfast Tin Soldier (1953)

Skipper John's Cook (1951)

Henry, Fisherman: A Story of the Virgin Islands (1949)

Stone Soup: An Old Tale (1947)

The Little Carousel (1946)

Brown's Major Literary Awards

1992 Laura Ingalls Wilder Award

1983 Caldecott Medal
Shadow

1974 Boston Globe–Horn Book Picture Book Honor Book
All Butterflies

1962 Caldecott Medal
Once a Mouse

1955 Caldecott Medal
Cinderella

1954 Caldecott Honor Book
The Steadfast Tin Soldier

1953 Caldecott Honor Book
Puss in Boots

1952 Caldecott Honor Book
Skipper John's Cook

1951 Caldecott Honor Book
Dick Whittington and His Cat

1950 Caldecott Honor Book
Henry, Fisherman: A Story of the Virgin Islands

1948 Caldecott Honor Book
Stone Soup: An Old Tale

Stone Soup: An Old Tale. Finally, in 1948, Brown quit her library job to be a full-time illustrator. Since then, she has illustrated many of her own adaptations of traditional tales, as well as books written by other people.

Brown has traveled widely and has studied the local folk traditions of several different countries. Many of her trips have led to illustrated books. After visiting the Virgin Islands, she wrote *Henry, Fisherman: A Story of the Virgin Islands*. A trip to Hawaii inspired *Backbone of the King: The Story of Paka'a and His Son Ku*. After a journey to East Africa, she got the idea for *Shadow*, which is based on African folklore. Later, she wrote *How the Ostrich Got Its Long Neck: A Tale from the Akamba of Kenya.*

Brown uses many different art techniques, including woodcuts, pen-and-ink drawings, and collages. She always chooses the method that best illustrates the particular story. Brown currently lives in Laguna Hills, California.

> *"Before starting to make the book, an artist must be sure the story is worth the time, his time and love spent in illustrating it, and the child's time to be spent in looking at it."*

WHERE TO FIND OUT MORE ABOUT MARCIA BROWN

BOOKS

Brown, Marcia. *Lotus Seeds: Children, Pictures and Books.* New York: C. Scribner's Sons, 1986.

McElmeel, Sharron L. *100 Most Popular Picture Book Authors and Illustrators: Biographical Sketches and Bibliographies.* Englewood, Colo.: Libraries Unlimited, 2000.

Rockman, Connie C., ed. *The Ninth Book of Junior Authors and Illustrators.* New York: H. W. Wilson Company, 2004.

Silvey, Anita, ed. *The Essential Guide to Children's Books and Their Creators.* Boston: Houghton Mifflin Company, 2002.

WEB SITES

ENCYCLOPEDIA BRITANNICA
http://www.britannica.com/ebi/article-9318152?tocId=9318152
To read a short biography of Marcia Brown

THE HORN BOOK
http://www.hbook.com/exhibit/brownbio.html
For a biography of the author

IN 1953, BROWN TAUGHT PUPPETRY AT THE UNIVERSITY COLLEGE OF THE WEST INDIES IN KINGSTON, JAMAICA.

Margaret Wise Brown

Born: May 23, 1910
Died: November 13, 1952

It is something of a cliché to say that writers lead extravagant, eccentric lives. But for Margaret Wise Brown, the cliché was a reality. With the royalties from her first picture book, she bought out the entire stock of a flower stall, scattered the flowers around her house, and threw a party! She believed that the lives of real people, in real settings, were more interesting than the folktales popular among children's authors. And it might just be that her own life was stranger than many a fictional tale.

Margaret Wise Brown was born in Brooklyn, New York, on May 23, 1910, at a time when delivery trucks had not yet put horses out of work. Her home was located next to New York's East River, and her earliest memories were the clop-clop of horses' hooves, the smell of

MARGARET WISE BROWN AND HER FRIENDS STARTED A SOCIAL CLUB CALLED THE BIRD BRAIN SOCIETY. ACCORDING TO ITS RULES, ANY MEMBER COULD DECLARE THAT IT WAS CHRISTMAS, AND THE OTHER MEMBERS GATHERED TOGETHER TO CELEBRATE.

tar from fishermen's ropes, and the sight of boats from around the world docking in New York Harbor. Her father earned his living making rope for the boats.

From a young age, Margaret believed that the children's stories she read were true. She could never quite understand why an author put his or her name on them. Why did it matter who wrote them if they were true stories? Later in life, she felt the same way and often used pen names instead of her own.

> *"I wish I could write a story that would seem absolutely true to the child who hears it and to myself."*

Brown attended Hollins College in Virginia and then the Writers Laboratory of the Bureau of Educational Experiments (later known as the Bank Street College of Education) in New York City. The school has become famous for studying the way children learn, and its style perfectly suited Brown. She taught special writing classes for children and encouraged them to talk about what interested them. She discovered that they too thought that real life was full of amusing incidents of all sorts.

Working as an editor for publisher William R. Scott, Brown guided children's books through to publication. But her head buzzed with stories of her own, and soon she was sending a flood of stories to different publishers. They were simple bedtime stories about puppies and pajama-clad bunnies.

———

MARGARET WISE BROWN WROTE THE TEXT FOR THE 1947 CALDECOTT WINNER *GOODNIGHT MOON*, ILLUSTRATED BY LEONARD WEISGARD, UNDER THE NAME GOLDEN MACDONALD.

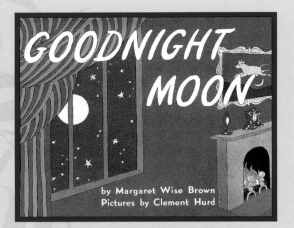

A Selected Bibliography of Brown's Work

The Good Little Bad Little Pig (2002)
Sheep Don't Count Sheep (2002)
The Dirty Little Boy (2001)
A Child Is Born (2000)
My World (1999)
I Like Stars (1998)
The Sleepy Men (1996)
Animals in the Snow (1995)
The Whispering Rabbit (1992)
Big Red Barn (1956)
Home for a Bunny (1956)
Willie's Adventures: Three Stories (1954)
The Quiet Noisy Book (1950)
A Pussycat's Christmas (1949)
Two Little Trains (1949)
The Golden Egg Book (1947)
Goodnight Moon (1947)
The Little Island (1947)
Little Fur Family (1946)
Red Light, Green Light (1944)
Little Chicken (1943)
The Runaway Bunny (1942)
Baby Animals (1941)
The Seashore Noisy Book (1941)

With the money she was paid for her books, Margaret Wise Brown indulged her whims. She was often seen walking her poodles in the streets of New York City. She frequently flew to Europe and entertained lavishly. She dated Prince Juan Carlos of Spain and befriended the famous screen actor John Barrymore and his wife. She bought a house in Maine, which she named Only House. It had no electricity, so she kept the wine, milk, and butter on labeled ropes dangling in the well outside to keep cool.

Margaret Wise Brown loved this way of life. She retained the imagination of a child and made life seem fun and unpredictable. At the age of forty-two, she

kicked up her leg to show a
doctor how well she was feeling.
The kick caused an embolism—a
blockage in a blood vessel—and
she died on November 13, 1952.
Her ashes were scattered off the
coast of Maine near Only House.

> *"One can but hope to make a child laugh or feel clear and happy-headed as he follows the simple rhythm to its logical end. It can jog him with the unexpected and comfort him with the familiar, lift him for a few minutes from his own problems."*

WHERE TO FIND OUT MORE ABOUT MARGARET WISE BROWN

BOOKS

Brown, Margaret W. *The Days before Now: An Autobiographical Note.* New York: Simon & Schuster Books for Young Readers, 1994.

Greene, Carol. *Margaret Wise Brown: Author of Goodnight Moon.* Chicago: Childrens Press, 1993.

Silvey, Anita, ed. *The Essential Guide to Children's Books and Their Creators.* Boston: Houghton Mifflin Company, 2002.

WEB SITE

HARPER COLLINS
http://www.harperchildrens.com/authorintro/index.asp?authorid=11849
Featuring a biography and booklist

MARGARET WISE BROWN HOME PAGE
http://www.margaretwisebrown.com/
For a biography of Margaret Wise Brown, plus a booklist and photos

BROWN WROTE UNDER MANY NAMES, SUCH AS TIMOTHY HAY, GOLDEN MACDONALD, AND KAINTUCK BROWN. HER COLLABORATIONS WITH EDITH THACHER HURD ARE PUBLISHED UNDER THE NAME JUNIPER SAGE.

Anthony Browne

Born: September 11, 1946

nthony Browne was born on September 11, 1946, in Sheffield, England. His parents ran a pub there called the Brinkliffe Oaks Hotel. Anthony loved to draw as a child. After high school, he went to an art college. He didn't like the school much, however. At one point, he had to spend three weeks drawing matches. He would drop a handful of matches on the tabletop, draw them exactly, then pick them up and draw them again.

Browne soon left the school and decided to become a medical illustrator instead. He applied for a training program but didn't get in. He was able to find a job as an assistant illustrator at Manchester Royal Infirmary. At the infirmary, Browne watched operations and drew pictures of them for

BROWNE LIKES TO HIDE SECRET IMAGES IN HIS ILLUSTRATIONS. FOR EXAMPLE, IF YOU LOOK CLOSELY AT THE PICTURES IN *THE TUNNEL*, YOU'LL NOTICE THAT ONE OF THEM CONTAINS A GORILLA THAT HAS NOTHING TO DO WITH THE STORY.

medical students to study. He says the experience taught him to use watercolors (his favorite medium) with great control. Also, "I learned to tell stories in pictures," he explains.

Browne tried other jobs. He taught art and worked at an advertising agency. He also spent fifteen years at a greeting-card company. Eventually he wanted to try his hand at something new. The owner of the card company introduced him to some book publishers.

Browne's first book wasn't successful, but he met an editor who taught him the craft of creating picture books. He tried again and soon published his first picture book, *Through the Magic Mirror.*

A Selected Bibliography of Browne's Work

Silly Billy (2006)
Into the Forest (2004)
The Shape Game (2003)
Animal Fair (2002)
My Dad (2000)
Willy's Pictures (2000)
Voices in the Park (1998)
Willy the Dreamer (1998)
Willy the Wizard (1995)
Zoo (1992)
Willy and Hugh (1991)
Things I Like (1989)
The Tunnel (1989)
I Like Books (1988)
Piggybook (1986)
Willy the Wimp (1984)
Gorilla (1983)
Hansel and Gretel (1981)
Bear Hunt (1980)
Through the Magic Mirror (1977)

Browne's Major Literary Awards

2004 Boston Globe–Horn Picture Book Honor Book
   The Shape Game

2000 Hans Christian Andersen Medal for Illustrators

1992 Kate Greenaway Medal
   Zoo

1986 Boston Globe–Horn Book Picture Book Honor Book
1983 Kate Greenaway Medal
   Gorilla

In Browne's mirror world, things don't work quite as they do in the real world. Mice chase cats, and dogs walk people. Though the pictures use a realistic style, they show bizarre events. In the world of art, a mixture of the real and the fantastic is called surrealism. It is one of Anthony Browne's favorite art forms.

> *"I was terrified of circuses and was carried screaming from the movie* Pinocchio *when I was two or three. Looking back, I was quite the wimp."*

"I think one of the things the surrealists were trying to do was to see things fresh for the first time," he says. "They would put two very ordinary objects together in an unusual place and create the feeling of looking at that object for the first time. . . . That, of course, is how children are looking at things, so there is a connection and I think that in some ways children have a surrealist view of the world. I know I did as a child."

If Anthony Browne has a trademark, though, it is the gorillas and apes that appear in so many of his books. Browne loves gorillas. "To look at one of them is to look at ourselves," he says. "But they are not quite like us—there's just that slight odd difference."

In his book *Gorilla,* a lonely girl dreams that a toy gorilla becomes real and befriends her. Six of Browne's books star one of his favorite characters—Willy the chimpanzee. One of the Willy books, *Willy's Pictures,*

ANTHONY BROWNE'S FIRST GORILLA WAS ON A BIRTHDAY CARD.
IT SHOWED A FIERCE-LOOKING GORILLA HOLDING A TEDDY BEAR.
"IN A WAY," HE SAYS, "I'VE BEEN REPEATING THAT IDEA EVER SINCE."

combines Browne's love of art with his love of apes. Willy paints his own versions of famous pictures, but paints primates where the people should be. For example, Willy paints Botticelli's masterpiece, *Birth of Venus.* Instead of a goddess standing on a giant seashell, there's a gorilla in a shower cap! Browne has even done a gorilla picture book for adults, retelling the story of King Kong.

> *"For me, planning a picture book is like planning a film, and the structure of the book is a combination of close-ups and long shots, and my feelings about these reflect the size of the picture."*

In 2000, Browne won the Hans Christian Andersen Medal for Illustrators, one of the highest awards in children's literature. He was the first British illustrator to win that medal in more than thirty-five years.

WHERE TO FIND OUT MORE ABOUT ANTHONY BROWNE

BOOKS

McElmeel, Sharron L. *100 Most Popular Picture Book Authors and Illustrators: Biographical Sketches and Bibliographies.* Englewood, Colo.: Libraries Unlimited, 2000.

Silvey, Anita, ed. *The Essential Guide to Children's Books and Their Creators.* Boston: Houghton Mifflin, 2002.

WEB SITE

WALKER BOOKS: ANTHONY BROWNE
http://www.walkerbooks.co.uk/Anthony-Browne
To read a biography of Anthony Browne and to explore his many books

SOMEONE ONCE ASKED BROWNE WHAT WAS THE FIRST PIECE OF ART HE WAS COMPLETELY SATISFIED WITH. HIS ANSWER: A DRAWING OF A DISSECTED RAT HE DREW WHEN HE WAS APPLYING TO TAKE CLASSES TO BECOME A MEDICAL ILLUSTRATOR.

Joseph Bruchac

Born: October 16, 1942

Storytelling is an important part of Joseph Bruchac's Abenaki heritage. As a young boy, he listened to people tell Native American tales. He loved hearing these tales and sharing them with other children. His passion for storytelling and his Native American heritage have made Bruchac a successful and popular author of books for children and young people. He has written poetry, novels, picture books, and Native American tales. Some of his best-known books include *Fox Song, Dawn Land,* and *The Girl Who Married the Moon: Stories from Native North America.*

Joseph Bruchac was born on October 16, 1942. He grew up in Greenfield Center, New York, a small town near the Adirondack

ALONG WITH HIS SISTER AND TWO SONS, BRUCHAC PERFORMS IN A MUSICAL GROUP CALLED THE DAWNLAND SINGERS. THEY PERFORM TRADITIONAL NATIVE AMERICAN MUSIC AND WRITE THEIR OWN SONGS.

Mountains. Joseph lived with his grandparents, who ran a small general store. He liked to help in the store and to listen to the stories the local farmers and lumberjacks told.

Joseph's grandmother was a graduate of law school. She was very intelligent and shared her love of reading with her grandson. She made sure that he always had books to read. His grandfather came from a Native American family. Even though his grandfather could barely read or write,

> *"I like being a writer because it is a way to share the things I care about with other people. It's great to be able to communicate this way. In some ways, it is the kind of joy that a teacher gets."*

Joseph learned a great deal from him. He taught Joseph how to appreciate the outdoors and love animals.

Joseph was a good student and did well in literature and science courses. He always thought about being a writer when he grew up. When he finished high school, he went to Cornell University to study wildlife conservation.

Then, in college, he took a creative writing class. This class inspired his interest in poetry. He graduated with a degree in English literature. After finishing college in 1966, he went to Africa to work as a teacher.

BRUCHAC HAS TAUGHT CREATIVE WRITING AND LITERATURE CLASSES AT
A SMALL COLLEGE IN NEW YORK. HE ALSO BEGAN A CREATIVE
WRITING PROGRAM FOR PRISON INMATES.

GLUSKABE AND THE FOUR WISHES

RETOLD BY *Joseph Bruchac*
ILLUSTRATED BY *Christine Nyburg Shrader*

A Selected Bibliography of Bruchac's Work

Return of Skeleton Man (2006)

Whisper in the Dark (2005)

Jim Thorpe's Bright Path (2004)

Warriors (2003)

Navajo Long Walk: The Tragic Story of a Proud People's Forced March from Their Homeland (2002)

Skeleton Man (2001)

Pushing Up the Sky: Seven Native American Plays for Children (2000)

The Heart of a Chief (1998)

Bowman's Store: A Journey to Myself (1997)

Eagle Song (1997)

Children of the Longhouse (1996)

The Boy Who Lived with the Bears: And Other Iroquois Stories (1995)

Gluskabe and the Four Wishes (1995)

The Story of the Milky Way: A Cherokee Tale (1995)

A Boy Called Slow: The True Story of Sitting Bull (1994)

The Girl Who Married the Moon: Stories from Native North America (1994)

Dawn Land (1993)

Fox Song (1993)

The First Strawberries: A Cherokee Story (1993)

Flying with the Eagle, Racing the Great Bear: Stories from Native North America (1993)

Turkey Brother and Other Tales: Iroquois Folk Stories (1975)

Indian Mountain and Other Poems (1971)

Bruchac's Major Literary Awards

2005 Carter G. Woodson Book Award
   Jim Thorpe's Bright Path

1996 Boston Globe–Horn Book Nonfiction Honor Book
   The Boy Who Lived with the Bears: And Other Iroquois Stories

After living in Africa for three years, Bruchac and his family moved back to New York. They moved into the same house he had lived in as a boy with his grandparents. As his children were growing up, Bruchac told them stories from their Native American heritage. He also worked at writing his own poems and stories.

Bruchac's first book of poetry, *Indian Mountain and Other Poems,* was published in 1971. Since that time, he has published more than seventy books for children and young people. He has contributed poems and stories to more than 500 publications. Bruchac and his wife also founded a small publishing company.

Joseph Bruchac still lives in the house he was raised in. Along with writing and editing children's books, Bruchac travels throughout the world as a storyteller.

> *"I believe that poetry is as much a part of human beings as is breath—and that, like breath, poetry links us to all other living things and is meant to be shared."*

WHERE TO FIND OUT MORE ABOUT JOSEPH BRUCHAC

BOOKS

Bruchac, Joseph. *Bowman's Store: A Journey to Myself.* New York: Dial Books, 1997.

Champagne, Duane, ed. *The Native North American Almanac.* Detroit: Visible Ink Press, 1994.

Silvey, Anita, ed. *The Essential Guide to Children's Books and Their Creators.* Boston: Houghton Mifflin Company, 2002.

Something about the Author. Vol. 89. Detroit: Gale Research, 1997.

WEB SITES

CHILDREN'S LITERATURE
http://www.childrenslit.com/f_bruchac.html
To read a biographical sketch and reviews of his works

JOSEPH BRUCHAC HOME PAGE
http://www.josephbruchac.com/
To learn more about Joseph Bruchac and for information on how to contact him

---

BRUCHAC'S TWO SISTERS ARE WRITERS. ONE SISTER IS AN EDITOR AND WRITES SCREENPLAYS. THE OTHER SISTER WRITES POETRY AND HISTORICAL PIECES.

Jean de Brunhoff
Laurent de Brunhoff

Born: December 9, 1899   Died: October 16, 1937 (Jean)
Born: August 30, 1925 (Laurent)

Babar the Elephant has become one of the best-known characters in children's literature since he was introduced in 1931. Jean de Brunhoff and his son Laurent (pictured right) wrote and illustrated dozens of books about this popular character.

Jean de Brunhoff was born on December 9, 1899, in Paris, France. His father published art magazines, and Jean inherited his love of art. Jean studied at an art school in Paris before joining the French army. As a soldier, he fought in World War I (1914–1918) for a short time. When he got out of the army, he continued to study art and work with a professional artist in Paris.

———

JEAN DE BRUNHOFF SPENT NEARLY THE LAST TWO YEARS OF HIS LIFE IN A HOSPITAL BECAUSE HE WAS SUFFERING FROM TUBERCULOSIS. HE CONTINUED TO WRITE STORIES WHILE IN THE HOSPITAL AND MAILED THEM TO HIS CHILDREN.

Brunhoff became a well-known painter in France. Many of his portrait and still-life paintings were displayed in museums. In 1924, he married Cécile Sabourand, and the couple had three sons. Cécile told the boys stories about a little elephant. The boys repeated these stories to their father. He decided to draw pictures and created his own story about the elephant he named Babar.

> *"My father never had it in mind to write a book for children. He was a painter, and it just happened one day that my mother narrated a story about a little elephant to us."*
> —*Laurent de Brunhoff*

Brunhoff's story excited his friends and relatives. They told him he should publish it as a children's book. In 1931, his first book, *Histoire de Babar,* was published in French. It was later translated into English and published as *The Story of Babar.* Brunhoff went on to write and illustrate seven more books about Babar before he died of tuberculosis in 1937.

When he became an adult, Brunhoff's oldest son, Laurent, decided to continue his father's work on the Babar books. Laurent had been born on August 30, 1925, in Paris. Like his father, he studied art and became an accomplished painter. His paintings and illustra-

TWO BOOKS WRITTEN AND ILLUSTRATED BY JEAN DE BRUNHOFF
—*BABAR AND HIS CHILDREN* AND *BABAR AND FATHER CHRISTMAS*—
WERE PUBLISHED AFTER HIS DEATH.

A Selected Bibliography of the Brunhoffs' Work

Babar's World Tour (2005)

Babar's Rescue (2004)

Babar's Yoga for Elephants (2002)

Babar and the Succotash Bird (2000)

Babar's Peekaboo Fair (1993)

Babar's Book of Color (1984)

Babar's ABC (1983)

Babar Visits Another Planet (1972)

Babar and the Doctor (1971)

Gregory and Lady Turtle in the Valley of the Music Trees (1971)

Anatole and His Donkey (1963)

Serafina the Giraffe (1961)

Babar's Fair (1956)

Babar and Zephir (1942)

Babar and Father Christmas (1940)

Babar and His Children (1938)

Babar the King (1935)

The Story of Babar, the Little Elephant (1933)

tions have been displayed in museums in the United States and Europe.

Laurent de Brunhoff finished the Babar stories that his father had started. He then created Babar stories of his own. His first Babar book was published in 1946. Since then, he has created more than forty books for children.

In Laurent de Brunhoff's books, Babar has gone camping, created paintings, and even traveled to other planets. Brunhoff has also written books that have helped children learn the alphabet, colors, and numbers.

Along with the many Babar books, Brunhoff has created books with other animal characters. These books include *Serafina the*

Giraffe, Gregory and Lady Turtle in the Valley of the Music Trees, and *Anatole and His Donkey.* Many of Brunhoff's books were written in French and then translated into English.

Brunhoff has also been involved in creating television shows and movies about Babar. He lives in New York and Key West, Florida, and continues to write and illustrate children's books.

> *"I love children; they are always ready to follow you into a dream. For them there is no border between dream and reality."*
> —*Laurent de Brunhoff*

WHERE TO FIND OUT MORE ABOUT JEAN AND LAURENT DE BRUNHOFF

BOOKS

Hildebrand, Ann M. *Jean and Laurent de Brunhoff.* New York: Twayne, 1991.

Silvey, Anita, ed. *The Essential Guide to Children's Books and Their Creators.* Boston: Houghton Mifflin Company, 2002.

Weber, Nicholas Fox. *The Art of Babar.* New York: Abrams, 1989.

WEB SITES

FIRST PERSON BOOK PAGE
http://www.bookpage.com/0009bp/laurent_de_brunhoff.html
To read an interview with Laurent de Brunhoff

WELCOME BABAR FANS!
http://www.angelfire.com/art/babar/
For biographical information on Jean and Laurent de Brunhoff, booklists, and a virtual museum of artwork related to Babar

---

BABAR: THE MOVIE WAS RELEASED IN 1989. IT WAS BASED ON CHARACTERS FROM THE BRUNHOFFS' BOOKS. A TELEVISION SERIES AND OTHER MOVIES FEATURING BABAR HAVE ALSO BEEN PRODUCED.

Ashley Bryan

Born: July 13, 1923

When author and illustrator Ashley Bryan speaks to the public, he is as dynamic as his vibrant, colorful art. He's constantly in motion—waving his hands, tapping his feet, and saying his words in a singsong, catchy rhythm. Bryan has illustrated more than thirty children's books. Most of them are tales and poems he has written, retold, or

compiled. Some of Bryan's best-loved works are retellings of traditional West African folktales. They are stories of tricksters, magical creatures, and cunning and foolish animals. Bryan uses a lively, rhythmic style in his writing that is similar to the word patterns and repetitions found in African storytelling.

Bryan's African American heritage inspires much of his work. His parents were immigrants from the island of Antigua in the West Indies. They settled in New York City, and Ashley was born there in 1923. He

WHEN ASHLEY WAS A LITTLE BOY, HE ENJOYED MAKING BOOKS FOR HIS FAMILY AND FRIENDS. HE WROTE THE STORIES, DREW THE PICTURES, AND BOUND THE BOOKS BY HAND.

and his five siblings grew up in an African American community in the Bronx neighborhood.

The Bryan kids loved to read, but their parents could not afford to buy them books. America was in the grip of the Great Depression at that time, and money was tight. Ashley and his siblings didn't let that stop them—they brought home stacks of books from their local public library. They proudly displayed these books on bookshelves they built out of orange crates. Ashley created his first book, an illustrated alphabet book, in kindergarten.

After high school, Bryan earned a scholarship to the Cooper Union School of Art in New York City. His schooling

A Selected Bibliography of Bryan's Work

Beautiful Blackbird (2004)

A Nest Full of Stars (Illustrations only, 2004)

How God Fix Jonah (Illustrations only, 2000)

The Night Has Ears (1999)

Ashley Bryan's African Tales, Uh-Huh (1998)

Carol of the Brown King: Nativity Poems (Illustrations only, 1998)

The House with No Door: African Riddle-Poems (Illustrations only, 1998)

Ashley Bryan's ABC of African-American Poetry (1997)

The Sun Is So Quiet (Illustrations only, 1996)

The Story of Lightning and Thunder (1993)

Sing to the Sun (1992)

Turtle Knows Your Name (1989)

All Night, All Day: A Child's First Book of African-American Spirituals (1988)

Sh-ko and His Eight Wicked Brothers (Writing only, 1988)

What a Morning! The Christmas Story in Black Spirituals (1987)

Lion and the Ostrich Chicks and Other African Folk Tales (1986)

The Cat's Purr (1985)

I Am Going to Sing: Black American Spirituals (1982)

Beat the Story-Drum, Pum-Pum (1980)

I Greet the Dawn (Illustrations only, 1978)

The Dancing Granny (1977)

The Adventures of Aku (1976)

The Ox of the Wonderful Horns and Other African Folktales (1971)

Moon, for What Do You Wait? (Illustrations only, 1967)

Bryan's Major Literary Awards

2004 Coretta Scott King Illustrator Award
Beautiful Blackbird

1998 Coretta Scott King Illustrator Honor Book
Ashley Bryan's ABC of African-American Poetry

1992 Coretta Scott King Illustrator Honor Book
All Night, All Day: A Child's First Book of African-American Spirituals

1988 Coretta Scott King Illustrator Honor Book
What a Morning! The Christmas Story in Black Spirituals

1987 Coretta Scott King Author Honor Book
1987 Coretta Scott King Illustrator Honor Book
Lion and the Ostrich Chicks and Other African Folk Tales

1983 Coretta Scott King Illustrator Honor Book
I'm Going to Sing: Black American Spirituals

1981 Coretta Scott King Illustrator Award
Beat the Story-Drum, Pum-Pum

was interrupted, though, while he served in World War II (1939–1945).
After the war, he completed his studies at Cooper Union and went on to
major in philosophy at Columbia University in New York City. He also
won a Fulbright scholarship to study art in Europe in
1950. Soon, Bryan began working as an illustrator.

> *"Be strongly rooted in who you are—your people and what they have had to offer—then reach out and draw upon the gifts of other peoples of the world."*

One day in the 1960s, Bryan had a visit from
Jean Karl, an editor at Atheneum Books. Karl had
heard about some colorful, hand-stitched books Bryan
was making. After seeing them for herself, she signed
Bryan to his first book contract. *Moon, for What Do
You Wait?*—a collection of East Indian poetry—was
published in 1967.

As Bryan gained fame as an illustrator, he never forgot the lack of
African American characters in the books he read as a child. He believes it's
important for African American children to hear stories and see illustrations
that remind them of their heritage. That's why Bryan enjoys sharing
African folktales with kids. He also focuses on spiritual hymns and poetry
by African American authors such as Langston Hughes. Among the many
prizes and honors Bryan has received are the Coretta Scott King Award and
the Arbuthnot Prize, an international award for lifetime achievement in
children's literature.

DURING WORLD WAR II, BRYAN JOINED THE ARMY AND SERVED IN FRANCE. EVEN
DURING HIS TIME AS A SOLDIER, HE NEVER STOPPED SKETCHING. BRYAN WOULD
STASH HIS DRAWING PAPER UNDER HIS HELMET TO KEEP IT DRY!

Bryan also taught art for many years. From 1973 to 1985, he worked at various colleges, including Queens College in New York City; Lafayette College in Easton, Pennsylvania; and Dartmouth College in Hanover, New Hampshire. Now he lives and works in his home on Little Cranberry Island, off the coast of Maine.

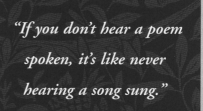

"If you don't hear a poem spoken, it's like never hearing a song sung."

WHERE TO FIND OUT MORE ABOUT ASHLEY BRYAN

BOOKS

Kovacs, Deborah, and James Preller. *Meet the Authors and Illustrators: 60 Creators of Favorite Children's Books Talk About Their Work.* New York: Scholastic Professional Books, 1991.

McElmeel, Sharron L. *100 Most Popular Picture Book Authors and Illustrators: Biographical Sketches and Bibliographies.* Englewood, Colo.: Libraries Unlimited, 2000.

Silvey, Anita, ed. *The Essential Guide to Children's Books and Their Creators.* Boston: Houghton Mifflin Company, 2002.

WEB SITES

THE CHILDREN'S BOOK COUNCIL
http://www.cbcbooks.org/cbcmagazine/meet/ashleybryan.html
To read an article by the author, a brief biography, a book list with awards

LIBRARY OF CONGRESS—NATIONAL BOOK FESTIVAL
http://www.loc.gov/bookfest/2002/bryan.html
For a biography and a small list of books

READING FUNDAMENTAL—INTRODUCING ILLUSTRATORS
http://www.washingtonpost.com/wp-srv/style/features/bryan.htm
To read an article about Ashley Bryan with personal quotes

BRYAN'S HOBBIES INCLUDE MAKING PUPPETS AND COLLECTING TOYS.

INDEX